# FROM SYMPTOM TO REALITY
IN MODERN HISTORY

RUDOLF STEINER

# FROM SYMPTOM TO REALITY IN MODERN HISTORY

*Nine lectures given in Dornach from 18th October to 3rd November, 1918*

Translated by A. H. Parker

RUDOLF STEINER PRESS
35 Park Road, London NW1 6XT

First English Edition, 1976

Translated from shorthand reports unrevised by the lecturer. In the Complete Edition of the works of Rudolf Steiner the volume containing the original German text is entitled: *Geschichtliche Symptomatologie*. (No. 185)

This English edition is published by permission of the *Rudolf Steiner-Nachlassverwaltung*, Dornach, Switzerland.

This translation

© Rudolf Steiner Press, London, 1976

ISBN 0 85440 298 5

MADE AND PRINTED IN GREAT BRITAIN BY
THE GARDEN CITY PRESS LIMITED
LETCHWORTH, HERTFORDSHIRE
SG6 1JS

The following lectures were given by Rudolf Steiner to audiences familiar with the general background of his anthroposophical teachings. He constantly emphasized the distinction between his written works and reports of lectures which were given as oral communications and were not originally intended for print. It should also be remembered that certain premises were taken for granted when the words were spoken. 'These premises,' Rudolf Steiner writes in his autobiography, 'include at the very least the anthroposophical knowledge of Man and of the Cosmos in its spiritual essence; also of what may be called "anthroposophical history", told as an outcome of research into the spiritual world.'

# CONTENTS

|  | page |
|---|---|
| Synopsis | 9 |

**LECTURE I** 18th October, 1918
*The birth of the Consciousness Soul*    17

**LECTURE II** 19th October, 1918
*Symptomatology of recent centuries*    44

**LECTURE III** 20th October, 1918
*Characteristics of historical symptoms in recent times*    71

**LECTURE IV** 25th October, 1918
*The historical significance of the scientific mode of thinking*    92

**LECTURE V** 26th October, 1918
*The supersensible element in the study of history*    113

**LECTURE VI** 27th October, 1918
*Brief reflections on the publication of the new edition of 'The Philosophy of Freedom'*    132

**LECTURE VII** 1st November, 1918
*Incidental reflections on the occasion of the new edition of 'Goethes Weltanschauung'*    157

**LECTURE VIII** 2nd November, 1918
*Religious impulses of the fifth post-Atlantean epoch*    184

**LECTURE IX** 3rd November, 1918
*The relation between the deeper European impulses and those of the present day*    203

*Notes*    237

*List of relevant literature*    245

# SYNOPSIS

## LECTURE I

*The birth of the Consciousness Soul*

Historical survey of our epoch from the standpoint of the Consciousness Soul. True reality lies concealed behind events. The great turning points in the evolution of mankind when the life of the soul passes from one stage of development to another stage. In the Middle Ages the universalist impulse of Catholicism was predominant and relied upon its power of suggestion. The conflict between the papacy and the empire—waning of Catholic power.

Symptoms of the new era—the removal of the pope to Avignon 1303, the suppression of the Order of the Templars, and the Mongol migrations. Existence of a more or less homogeneous complex which later gave birth to France and England. Joan of Arc and the emergence of nationalism, 1429. Nationalism as a unifying factor.

The conflict between Central and Eastern Empire leading to colonizing activity and the intermingling of the Slavonic and Teutonic peoples. The peasant revolts and the rise of Hapsburg power. Growth of towns between the thirteenth and fifteenth centuries with their specific urban outlook. Preparation of parliamentary government in England as a result of the civil wars. Birth of the impulse of the Consciousness Soul. The political and social structure of Russia based on tradition. The revolt of the self-reliant personality against the universalist impulse of Catholicism brought no new creative ideas. Hus, Savanarola, Calvin and Luther challenged traditional ideas, but were uncreative. The dawn of the Consciousness Soul signifies a new relationship to the creative ideas of the past.

The national impulse and the emancipation of the independent personality followed different paths in France and England. In France the national element is orientated towards man and leads to the Revolution of 1789; in England towards mankind and leads to liberalism. Here the personal element transcends nationalism and strives to embrace the whole world. Significance of the battle of Trafalgar. In North America about the 1780's the specifically French nuance, Romanism, is subverted by the Anglo-Saxon element and lost to the world. A personality characteristic of the rise of the Consciousness Soul is James I of England.

*From Symptom to Reality in Modern History*

LECTURE II

*Symptomatology of recent centuries*
Contradictions in the personalities of the epoch of the Consciousness Soul, e.g. James I. Loss of creative energy in this epoch. Increasing divergence between the French and English character. Consolidation of the state idea under Louis XIV, a consequence of the chaos of the Thirty Years' War. The emancipation of the personality and its chaotic expression in the French Revolution. Liberty, equality and fraternity must be rightly associated with the tripartite division of man. The Revolution was all soul without body, Napoleon all body without a soul. The seven year cycles in Napoleon's life. Purpose of the Consciousness Soul is to develop independence, self-reliance. The need to abandon old supports and work out one's religious faith. Potential dangers. Rome opposed to the development of the Consciousness Soul and wished to keep man at the level of the Intellectual Soul. The stifling of the aspiration to the Consciousness Soul by reviving traditions of a past epoch, e.g. Freemasonry and the impulses of the Egypto-Chaldaean epoch. The two streams of recent history: the chaotic search for liberty, equality and fraternity; the various Orders which seek to stifle the awakening of the Consciousness Soul for their own ends. Thus the impulse to transcend nationalism by the development of the personality was blunted. Liberalism which aimed at political enlightenment declined in the last third of the nineteenth century. Spirit and soul no longer active forces; the phenomenal world the sole reality. Socialism as one of the most significant symptoms of modern times. The three tenets of socialism—the materialist conception of history, the theory of surplus value and the theory of the class struggle—Marx, Engels and Lassalle. Birth of international socialism. Another symptom of our time: the creation of insoluble problems, e.g. Alsace.


LECTURE III

*Characteristics of historical symptoms in recent times*
The rise of socialism and its limitations. The significance of the scientific mode of thinking. Birth of the machine age. Colonizing activities dependent upon the achievements of natural science. The importance of colonization for the epoch of the Consciousness Soul. The impulse of the Consciousness Soul brings to an end the differentiation between men. The difference between observation of nature and knowledge derived from experimentation can be exploited technically. Technics introduce forces of death into social life. By reacting against technics man develops the Consciousness Soul. The relation between consciousness and the forces of death. The function of catabolic processes in man. Parliamentary

## Synopsis

government ends in the suppression of personality; democracy ends in egalitarianism.

The Masonic lodges and the mystery of birth and death. The impulses of the papacy are turned against Catholicism, cf. Garibaldi. The Byzantine tradition in Russian orthodoxy, a powerful force in opposition to the emancipation of the personality. Russia bears within it the seeds of the Spirit Self.

The meeting of Goethe and Soret in 1830. The controversy between Cuvier and Geoffrey de Saint Hilaire. The latter sees nature as a living organism, the former compares and classifies organisms. Thinking still active in sleep. What the Gods implanted in the instinctive life in early times must be replaced by supersensible knowledge. The conquests of modern science, etcetera must be transformed by insight into the supersensible. Man must open himself to the supersensible so that what his Spirit Self prepares may enter into his ego. Modern history fails to penetrate to spiritual realities, and modern medicine to symptoms of cosmic origin. Disease as a visitation from heaven. Relation between epidemics and the periodicity of sun spots.

## LECTURE IV

### *The historical significance of the scientific mode of thinking*

Difference between knowledge derived from observation of nature and from experimentation. Facts of history are symbols of an underlying reality. Development of the Consciousness Soul must be accompanied by receptivity to the spiritual. Importance of the October Revolution of 1917 in Russia for a co-operative life. The social revolutionaries, the Mensheviks, bereft of ideas. The Bolsheviks, the radical left wing of the Social Democratic party, take over; opposed to a spiritual *Weltanschauung*. Fruitful ideas could only spring from a spiritual outlook, but were rejected by the oppressed classes. The proletariat a product of the machine age and purely pragmatic in outlook. Cut off from nature, surrounded by a mechanized environment, it envisages the world and the social order as a vast machine.

Between 1860 and 1873 a tendency towards altrusim. The need to awaken an active interest in our fellow men. Importance of sickness and a positive attitude to life.

The forces of birth and death active throughout the life of man. In Graeco-Latin epoch they were evenly balanced in the early thirties of man's life. In epoch of Consciousness Soul, intellectual development ceases before middle life. Today we must consciously create and destroy, we must recognize the impermanence of things. Birth and death must be woven into our social life. In the fifth post-Atlantean epoch evil will

## From Symptom to Reality in Modern History

be developed in man and in the sixth epoch will be experienced externally. Christ destined to appear again in the etheric body in the fifth epoch. The Christ impulse born out of the forces of death. Through the forces of evil mankind will be led to a renewed experience of the Mystery of Golgotha.

### LECTURE V

*The supersensible element in the study of history*

Relationship of the Mystery of Evil to the Mystery of Death and the Mystery of Golgotha. Purpose of the forces which bring death to man is to endow him with the capacity to develop the Consciousness Soul. Forces of evil necessary for the development of the Consciousness Soul; they awaken in man a desire for the life of the spirit.

The need to develop a sympathetic understanding for others in the epoch of the Consciousness Soul in four domains. First, men will see each other differently in future. The role of art. Secondly, a new understanding will be developed. Men will be able to hear the soul through language and will experience a sensation of colour. Thirdly, they will experience in their respiration the emotional reactions of others. Respiration will adapt itself to the affective life of others. And fourthly, men will learn to 'digest' each other in the sphere of will. But all these forces will only be fully developed in the Jupiter, Venus and Vulcan periods.

Today it is necessary to overcome particularist tendencies. Man rebels against this; the spread of the doctrine of national self-determination, but this is opposed to the divinely ordered course of evolution.

The sterility of modern Masonry: difficulties of taking up Anthroposophy. Modern 'prophets' and the easy path to the spirit. A reminder of the four steps of future development and why the extreme left came to power in Russia.

### LECTURE VI

*Brief reflections on the publication of the new edition of 'The Philosophy of Freedom'*

Dr. Steiner's involvement in the impulses of the fifth post-Atlantean epoch. His invitation to Weimar and his collaboration in editing the Weimar edition of Goethe's works. Weimar as a centre of international scholars of repute.

Discussion of the first section of *The Philosophy of Freedom*. Necessary to establish the idea of freedom on a firm, scientific basis. The soul of man permeated by the cosmic process; modern scientific thinking is tied to the

*Synopsis*

phenomenal world and unable to arrive at a philosophy of freedom. The second section of the book deals with the reality of freedom which can become a driving force in social life. Plea for ethical individualism; we must overcome the constraint of natural laws and conventional moral norms.

Dr. Steiner moved to Berlin. Took over the review *Das Magazin* as platform for his ideas. Found some support from B. Tucker and J. H. Mackay. Opposition from his contemporaries, the Berlin professoriate. The vulgarity of Bölsche's ideas popular at the time. Further details of Berlin life—the Dreyfus affair, criticism of Max Halbe, friendship with O. E. Hartleben and severance from the *Magazin*.

Dr. Steiner's association with Berlin Workers' College. Socialist workers infected with positivism and Marxism. Freedom no place in the socialist programme. Rosa Luxembourg on 'Science and the Workers'. Failure of learned professions—their ideas no spiritual basis.

Invited to lecture before Berlin Theosophical Society. His association with the Theosophical movement and speech before congress in London chaired by Mrs. Besant. Found no support here for the ideas of *The Philosophy of Freedom*.

Need to grasp the idea and importance of ethical individualism, to develop a thinking freed from the tyranny of the senses, a disciplined scientific thinking combined with an insight into the spiritual world.

## LECTURE VII

*Incidental reflections on the occasion of the new edition of 'Goethes Weltanschauung'*

Reasons for choosing the name Goetheanum for the Anthroposophical Centre at Dornach. Dr. Steiner's early literary activity associated with Goethe and Goetheanism. Historical events and the lives of individuals as pointers: one must look beyond facts to ascertain their inner meaning. A desire for supersensible vision today, but unwillingness to undertake the necessary training. The law of causality and the destiny of Robert Hamerling.

The Austrian, German by descent and racial affiliation, and his strange position in Imperial Germany—different modes of apprehension, etcetera.

Steiner's formative years at Neudörfl. The problem of Cis-Leithania and trans-Leithania. His environment held little interest for him. Education in the Realschule at Wiener-Neustadt with emphasis on natural science. Brief comments on his teachers.

Outgrows the limited horizon of the Austrian background and turns towards the legacy of German culture and Goetheanism. Goetheanism the vital impulse for the modern epoch—it is a crystallization of divers impulses of the fifth post-Atlantean epoch. An isolated phenomenon and will never become popular. The spiritual impulses of the age remote from reality, cf. the churches and universities. R. Steiner's arrival in Weimar 1889. Influence of K. J. Schröer and H. Grimm. Schröer's work on Goethe not taken seriously by the universities. Goethe's significance for our time—his *Weltanschauung* rests on a scientific foundation; Goethe's intuitive perception of nature and his conception of man as an integral part of the cosmos. Goethe a universal genius—his phenomenal versatility. Purpose of the book, *Goethes Weltanschauung*, to awaken Steiner's contemporaries to a knowledge of the real Goethe. Goetheanism prepares the ground for spiritual science. *The Philosophy of Freedom* intended to serve the needs of the time and offer a challenge to the destructive forces acting against the spirit of the age. Steiner's work sets out to develop insight into, and understanding of what is needed, and to preserve the world from the havoc of Wilsonism.

## LECTURE VIII

*Religious impulses of the fifth post-Atlantean epoch*

Three currents of evolution are confluent in man. In the course of the post-Atlantean epoch man reaches physical maturity at an ever earlier age, e.g. in ancient India at the age of fifty, today at twenty-eight. Mankind as a whole at the present time develops as far as the stage of the Sentient Soul. In the second current of evolution the individual develops the Consciousness Soul. The third current of evolution is that of peoples or nations—the Italian people develops the Sentient Soul, the French the Intellectual Soul, and the English speaking peoples the Consciousness Soul.

Birth of the People of the Christ in the East in the ninth century. Differentiations of the Christ impulse in Europe. Russian people as vehicle for the revelation of the Christ impulse. The controversy between Photius and Pope Nicholas I.

Solovieff wished to spiritualize the material world. The second differentiation of the Christ impulse seen in the Church of Rome, which transformed the spiritual sovereignty of Christ into the temporal sovereignty of the Church.

Development of the Consciousness Soul leads to Reformist teachings, e.g. Luther, Zwingli, Calvin, etcetera. Conflict with Rome. The People of the Church. Jesuitism as the militia of the Counter Reformation. The spiritual exercises of Ignatius Loyola. Results of Jesuitism. Polarity of Goetheanism and Jesuitism.

# *Synopsis*

## LECTURE IX

*The relation between the deeper European impulses and those of the present day*
Interaction of the three currents of evolution—that of mankind as a whole, that of man as individual and that of the folk souls. Action of the Christ Impulse at three levels, cf. Wilhelm Meister and the picture gallery. Pictorial representation of (a) world history and the evolution of mankind, (b) the life of Christ up to the Last Supper, (c) from the Last Supper until His Death and Resurrection. The Grail atmosphere in Goethe's *Wilhelm Meister*. These three currents of evolution assume different forms, e.g. in Arianism and Athanasianism. The doctrinal dispute over the relationship of God the Father to Christ the Son. Ulfilas and his translation of the Bible. Victory of Athanasianism through Clovis and Charlemagne: the transition to Roman Catholicism.

The Celtic civilization in Europe: its survival in Wales. The Celts and the authoritarian, aristocratic structure of society, cf. King Arthur and his Knights. Amongst those still influenced by the Celts, Christ appears as a feudal lord as in the religious epic *Heliand*.

The People of the Lodges in W. Europe. Their relation to Jesuitism. The work of Herbert of Cherbury. Fruit of the 'Lodge' impulse was *Aufklärung* and the spirit of rationalism in all spheres. Christ only a teacher. Deism of the *Aufklärung* in Harnack. The Grail current and Goetheanism—its antithesis to the Arthurian current.

Goethe and the Consciousness Soul. Birth of socialism. Polarity of individualism and socialism. Aim of socialism—to realize fraternity in the social organism, liberty in the sphere of religion and equality in the domain of knowledge. Paul Ernst and his article on moral courage in the *Frankfurter Zeitung*.

## LECTURE I

In the course of these lectures I propose to make some important additions to the enquiry which I undertook here last week.* Our earlier investigation gave us a certain insight into the impulses which determine the recent evolution of mankind. What I now propose to add will emerge from a study of the various turning points in modern history. We will endeavour to study this recent history up to the moment when we shall see how the human soul at the present day is related to the universe, in respect of its evolution within the cosmos and of its inner development in relation to the divine and its ego development in relation to the spirit. I should like to show the connection between these things and the more or less everyday occurrences which are familiar to you. Therefore I will first take as my point of departure today—and the reasons for this will be apparent tomorrow and the day after tomorrow—the historical survey of the recent evolution of mankind which was to some extent the background to the observations on modern history, observations which I suggested in my public lecture in Zürich yesterday.†

From my earlier lectures in which I discussed analogous themes you already know that from the standpoint of spiritual science what is usually called history must be seen as a complex of symptoms. From this point of view what is usually taught as history, the substance of what is called history in the

* *Das Geschichtsleben der Menschheit*, Dornach, October, 1918. Lectures included in *Die Polarität von Dauer und Entwickelung im Menschenleben* (Bibl. Nr. 184).

† *Die Geschichte der Neuzeit im Lichte der Geisteswissenschaftlicher Forschung* 17th October, 1918 (included in Bibl. Nr. 73).

## From Symptom to Reality in Modern History

scholastic world, does not touch upon the really vital questions in the evolutionary history of mankind; it deals only with superficial symptoms. We must penetrate beneath the surface phenomena and uncover the deeper layer of meaning in events and then the true reality behind the evolution of mankind will be revealed. Whilst history usually studies historical events in isolation, we shall here consider them as concealing a deeper underlying reality which is revealed when they are studied in their true light.

A little reflection will show how absurd, for example, is the oft repeated assertion that modern man is the product of the past, and this remark invites us to study the history of this past. Recall for a moment the events of history as presented to you at school and ask yourself what influence they may have had, as history claims to show, upon your own sentient life, upon the constitution of your soul! But the study of the constitution of the soul in its present state of development is essential to the knowledge of man, to the knowledge of oneself. But history as usually presented does not favour this self knowledge. A limited self knowledge however is sometimes brought about indirectly. Yesterday, for example, a gentleman told me that he had been given three hours' detention because in class one day he had forgotten the date of the battle of Marathon. Clearly such an experience works upon the soul and so might contribute indirectly to a better understanding of the impulses which lead to self knowledge! But the way in which history treats of the battle of Marathon adds little to man's real understanding of himself. None the less, a symptomatology of history must take into account external facts, for the simple reason that by the study and evaluation of these external facts we can gain insight into what really takes place.

I will begin by tracing the main features of contemporary history. The history which we study at school usually be-

## Lecture I

gins with the discovery of America and the invention of gunpowder and opens, as you know, with the statement that the Middle Ages have drawn to a close and that we now stand on the threshold of the modern era. Now if such a study is to be fruitful, it is important to turn our attention especially to the real and fundamental changes in human evolution, to those decisive turning-points in history when the life of the soul passes from one stage of development to another stage. These moments of transition usually pass unnoticed because they are overlooked amid the tangled skein of events. Now we know from the purely anthroposophical point of view that the last great turning point in the history of civilization occurred in the early years of the fifteenth century, when the fifth post-Atlantean epoch began. The Greco-Latin epoch opened in 747 B.C. and lasted until the beginning of the fifteenth century which ushered in the fifth post-Atlantean epoch. Because people only take a superficial view of things they usually fail to recognize that, during this period, the whole of man's soul-life underwent modification. It is manifestly absurd to regard the sixteenth century simply as a continuation of the eleventh or twelfth centuries. People overlook the radical change that occurred towards the beginning of the fifteenth century and persisted in the subsequent years. This point in time is of course only approximate; but what is not approximate in life? Whenever one stage of evolution which is to some extent complete in itself passes over into another stage we must always speak of approximation. It is impossible to determine the precise moment when an individual arrives at puberty; the onset is gradual and then runs its course to full physical maturity. And the same applies, of course, to the year 1413 which marks the birth of the Consciousness Soul. The new consciousness develops gradually and does not immediately manifest itself everywhere in full maturity and with maximum vigour. We completely fail to understand historical change unless we give due consideration to the moment when events take on a new orientation.

When, looking back to the period before the fifteenth century, we wish to enquire into and compare the predominant condition of the human soul at that time with the progressive transformation of this psychic condition after the beginning of the fifteenth century, we cannot help turning our attention to the real situation which existed in civilised Europe throughout the whole of the Middle Ages and which was still intimately related to the whole psychic condition of the Greco-Latin epoch. I am referring to the form which Catholicism that was subject to the Papacy had gradually developed over the centuries out of the Roman Empire. We cannot understand Catholicism before the great turning point which marks the birth of modern times unless we bear in mind that it was a universalist impulse and that, as such, it spread far and wide. Now mediaeval society was hierarchically ordered; men were grouped according to social status, family connections; they were organized in craft and merchant guilds, etcetera. But all these social stratifications were indoctrinated with Catholicism, and in the form that Christianity had assumed under the impact of various impulses of which we shall learn more in the following lectures (and under the impact of those impulses which I mentioned in earlier lectures). The expansion of Catholicism was characterized by the form of Christianity which was decisively influenced by Rome in the way I have indicated.

The Catholicism which emanated from Rome and developed after its own fashion through the centuries was a universalist impulse, the most powerful force animating European civilization. But it counted upon a certain unconsciousness of the human soul, a susceptibility of the human

## Lecture I

soul to suggestionism. It counted upon those forces with which the human soul had been endowed for centuries when it was not yet fully conscious—(it has only become fully conscious in our present epoch). It counted upon those who were only at the stage of the Rational or Intellectual Soul and calculated that by its power of suggestion it could slowly implant into their affective life what it deemed to be useful. And amongst the educated classes—which consisted of the clergy for the most part—it counted upon a keen and critical intelligence which had not yet arrived at the stage of the Consciousness Soul. The development of theology as late as the thirteenth, fourteenth and fifteenth centuries showed that it relied upon a razor-sharp intelligence. But if you take the intelligence of today as the measure of man's intelligence you will never really understand what was meant by intelligence up to the fifteenth century. Up to that time intelligence was to some extent instinctive, it had not yet been impregnated with the Consciousness Soul. Mankind did not yet possess the capacity for independent reflection which came only with the development of the Consciousness Soul. None the less men displayed on occasions astonishing acumen to which many of the mediaeval disputations bear witness, for many of these disputations were debated with greater intelligence than the doctrinal disputes of later theology. But this was not the intelligence that was an expression of the Consciousness Soul, it was the intelligence which, in popular parlance, came from 'on high'; esoterically speaking it was a manifestation of the Angelos, a faculty not yet under man's control. Independent thinking became possible only when he achieved self dependence through the Consciousness Soul. When a universalist impulse is diffused in this way through the power of suggestion, as was the case with the Roman Papacy and everything associated with it in the structure of the Church, then it is much more the community, the Group Soul element,

*From Symptom to Reality in Modern History*

everything that is related to the Group Soul that is affected. And this spirit of self dependence also affected Catholicism, with the result that under the influence of certain impulses of contemporary history this universalist impulse of expanding Catholicism found in the Holy Roman Empire of the German nation its battering ram. We will discuss these matters from another standpoint later on. We see how the expansion of universal Roman Catholicism was prosecuted amid continuous conflict and contention with the Roman Empire. One need only refer to the period of the Carolingians and the Hohenstaufens[1] in the standard history books to find that the fundamental issue was the incorporation of Europe into a universal Christian church of Roman Catholic persuasion.

If we wish to have a clear understanding of these matters from the point of view of the dawning Consciousness Soul we must consider an important turning point which, symptomatically, reveals the waning of Catholic power which had dominated the Middle Ages. And this turning point in modern history is the transference of the Pope to Avignon in 1309.[2] Such a challenge to the papacy would formerly have been impossible and shows that mankind which formerly had been dominated by a universalist impulse now begins to undergo a transformation. That a king or an emperor could have entertained the idea of transferring the residence of the Pope from Rome to some other city would have been inconceivable in earlier times. In 1309 the matter was quickly dealt with—the Pope was transferred to Avignon and the next decades witnessed the endless quarrels between popes and anti-popes associated with this transference of the papal court. And a victim of this conflict within the Church was the Order of the Templars,[3] which had been loosely associated with the Papacy, though of course its relationship to Christianity was totally different. The Order was suppressed in 1312

*Lecture I*

shortly after the removal of the Pope to Avignon. This is a turning point in modern history and we must consider this turning point not only in respect of its factual content, but as a symptom, if we wish gradually to discover the reality concealed behind it.

Let us now turn our attention to other symptoms of a similar kind at the time of this turning point in history. As we survey the continent of Europe we are struck by the fact that its life, largely in the Eastern areas, is profoundly influenced by those events which operate in the course of history after the fashion of natural phenomena. I am referring to the continuous migrations, beginning with the Mongol invasions[4] in the not far distant past, which poured in from Asia and introduced an Asiatic element into Europe. When we link an event such as the transference of the Papacy to Avignon with these invasions from the East we establish important criteria for a symptomatology of history. Consider the following: in order to understand not the inward and spiritual, but the external and human tendencies and influences which were connected with the event of Avignon and prepare the ground for it, you need not look beyond a coherent complex of human acts and decisions. But you will find no such coherent pattern of events when you consider the time between the Mongol invasions and the later penetration of the Turks into Europe. But when studying any historical event, a complex of facts of this kind, you must consider the following if you really wish to arrive at a symptomatology of history.

Let us assume for the moment that here is Europe and here is Asia. The columns of the invading armies are advancing towards Europe. One of these columns, let us assume, has penetrated as far as this frontier. On the one side are the Mongols and later the Turks; on the other side the Europeans. When considering the event of

*From Symptom to Reality in Modern History*

Avignon you find a complex of acts and decisions taken by men. There is no such complex across the frontier. You have to consider two aspects, the one on this side of the frontier, the other on the other side. For the Europeans the Mongolian wave that sweeps across the frontier resembles a natural phenomenon of which one sees only the external effects. The invaders pour across the frontier, invade the neighbouring territory and harass the inhabitants; behind them lies a whole culture of the soul of

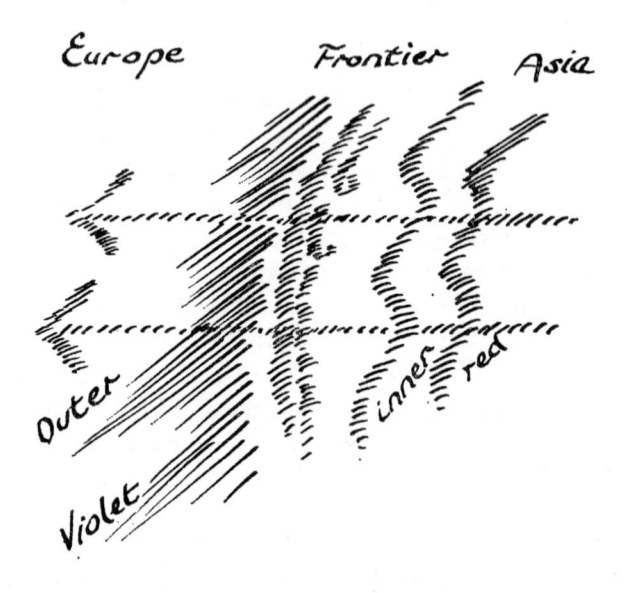

which they are the vehicle. Their own inner life lies behind the frontier. But this psychic life does not reach beyond the frontier which acts as a kind of sieve through which passes only energies akin to the elemental forces of nature. These two aspects—the inner aspect which is found amongst those who live behind this frontier and the aspect which shows only its external face to the Europeans—these are not

## Lecture I

to be found, of course, in the episode of Avignon, where everything forms a single complex, a composite whole. Now an occurrence such as these Asiatic invasions closely resembles what one sees in nature. Imagine you are looking at the world of nature ... You see the colours, you hear the sounds—but these are external trappings. Behind lies the spirit, behind are the elemental beings which are active up to the point where the frontier begins. (See diagram.) You see with your eyes, hear with your ears, you experience by touch—and behind lies the spirit which does not cross the frontier, does not manifest itself. Such is the situation in nature, but in history it is not quite the same, though somewhat similar. The psychic element behind history does not manifest itself, we see only its external appearance.

It is most important to bear in mind this strange intermediate zone, this no man's land, where peoples or races clash, revealing to each other only their external aspects—this strange intermediate zone (which must also be reckoned among the symptoms) between actual universal experience of the human soul such as we see in the event of Avignon and the genuine impressions of nature. All the historical twaddle which has come to the fore recently, and which has no idea of the operation of this intermediate zone, cannot arrive at a true history of civilization. For this reason, neither Buckle nor Ratzel[5] (I mention two historians of widely divergent outlook), could arrive at a true history of civilization because they started from the preconceived idea: of two events, if one follows from the other, then the later event must be considered as the effect and the earlier event the cause—the common sense view that is generally accepted.

When we consider this event as a symptomatic event in the recent evolution of mankind, then, as we shall see in later lectures, it will provide a bridge from the symptoms to reality.

*From Symptom to Reality in Modern History*

Now from the complex of facts we see emerging in the West of Europe a more or less homogeneous configuration at first, which later gives birth to France and England. Leaving aside for the moment the external elements such as the Channel, which is simply a geographical factor separating the two countries, it is difficult at first to distinguish between them. In the period when modern history begins French culture was widespread in England. English Kings extended their dominion to French territory, and members of the respective dynasties each laid claim to the throne of the other country. But at the same time we see emerging one thing, which throughout the Middle Ages was also associated with what the universalist impulse of Catholicism had to some extent relegated to the background. I mentioned a moment ago that at this time communities were already in existence; families were cemented by the blood-tie to which they clung tenaciously; men were organized in craft guilds or corporations, etcetera. All these organizations were permeated by the powerful and authoritative universalist Catholic impulse moulded by Rome which dominated them and set its seal upon them. And just as this Roman Catholic impulse had relegated the guilds and other corporate bodies to a subordinate role, so too national identity suffered the same fate. At the time when Roman Catholicism exercised its greatest dynamic power national identity was not regarded as the most important factor in the structure of the human soul. Consciousness of nationality now began to be looked upon as something vastly more important than it had been when Catholicism was all powerful. And significantly it manifested itself in those countries I have just mentioned. But whilst the general idea of nationhood was emerging in France and England an extremely significant differentiation was taking place at the same time. Whilst for centuries these countries had shared a common purpose, differences began

## Lecture I

to emerge in the fifteenth century. The first indications are seen in the appearance of Joan of Arc in 1429, a most important turning point in modern history. It was this appearance of Joan of Arc which gave the impetus—and if you consult the manuals of history you will see how important, powerful and continuous this impetus was—which led to the differentiation between the French and the English character.

Thus we see the emergence of nationalism as the architect of the community and at the same time this differentiation which is so significant for the evolution of modern mankind. This turning point is marked by the appearance of Joan of Arc in 1429. At the moment when the impulse of the Papacy is compelled to release from its clutches the population of Western Europe, at that moment the consciousness of nationality gathers momentum in the West and shapes its future. Do not allow yourselves to be misled in this matter. As history is presented today you can, of course, find in the past of every people or nation a consciousness of nationality. But you do not attach any importance to the potent influence of this force. Take, for example, the Slav peoples: under the influence of modern ideas and currents of thought they will of course trace back as far as possible the origin of their national sentiments and forces. But in the period of which we are speaking the national impulses were particularly active so that, in the territories I have just mentioned, there was an epoch when these impulses underwent a profound modification. And this is what matters. If we wish to apprehend reality we must make strenuous efforts to achieve objectivity. Another symptomatic fact which also reveals the emergence of the Consciousness Soul—like the one I have just mentioned—is the strange fashion in which the Italian national consciousness developed out of the levelling influence of the Papacy which, as we have seen, relegated the national impulse to a subordinate role, an

*From Symptom to Reality in Modern History*

influence which had hitherto pervaded the whole of Italy. Fundamentally it was the national impulse which emancipated the people of Italy from papal sovereignty at this time. All these facts are symptoms which are inherent in the epoch when, in Europe, the civilization of the Consciousness Soul seeks to emerge from the Civilization of the Rational and Intellectual Soul.

At the same time—we are anticipating of course—we see the beginning of the conflict between Central and Eastern Europe. What emerged from what I described as the 'battering ram' of the Papacy, from the Holy Roman Empire of the German nation, came into conflict with Slav expansionism.

The most diverse historical symptoms bear witness to this interaction between Central and Eastern Europe. In history one must not attach so much importance to princely families or personages as modern historians are wont to do. After all only a Wildenbruch[6] could throw dust in people's eyes by pretending that the farce played out between Louis the Pious and his sons had historical significance. Only a Wildenbruch could present these family feuds in his dramas as historically important. They have no more significance than any other domestic gossip; they have nothing to do with the evolution of mankind. It is only when we study the symptomatology of history that we develop a feeling for what is really important and what is relatively unimportant in the evolution of mankind. In modern times the conflict between Central and Eastern Europe has important implications. But in reality Ottokar's conflict with Rudolf[7] is only an indication; it is a pointer to what actually happened. On the other hand it is most important not to take a narrow view of this conflict. We must realize that, during this continuous confrontation, a colonizing activity began which carried the peasants from Central to Eastern Europe and in later years from the Rhine to Siebenbürgen. These peasant migrations, through

*Lecture I*

the mingling of Central and Eastern European elements, had a profound influence upon the later development of life in these areas. Thus the Slavs whose expansionist policy came into conflict with what had developed in Central Europe out of the Holy Roman Empire were continuously infiltrated by Central European colonists moving eastwards. And from this strange process emerged that which later became the Hapsburg power. But another consequence of this ferment in Europe was the formation of certain centres which developed a particular cast of mind within the urban communities. The main period when the towns throughout Europe developed their specifically urban outlook lies between the thirteenth and the fifteenth centuries. What I have described in a previous lecture* penetrated into these towns; in these towns men were able to develop their individual characteristics.

Now it is a remarkable and significant phenomenon that after the separate development of France and England, there emerged in England at this time, after slow and careful preparation, that which later became the system of parliamentary government in Europe. As a result of the long civil wars which lasted from 1452–1480, we see developing, amongst manifold external symptoms, the historical symptom of embryonic parliamentary government. When the era of the Consciousness Soul opened in the early fifteenth century people wanted to take their affairs into their own hands. They wanted to debate, to discuss, to have a say in future policies and to shape external events accordingly—or at least liked to imagine that they shaped events. This spirit of independence—as a result of the disastrous civil wars in the fifteenth century—developed in England out of that configuration which was markedly different from what had also

* *Die Geschichte des Mittelalters bis zu den grossen Erfindungen und Entdeckungen*, Berlin, October–December, 1904.

arisen in France under the influence of the national impulse. Parliamentary Government in England developed out of the national impulse. We must clearly recognize that, through the birth of parliamentary government as a consequence of the English civil wars in the fifteenth century, we see the interplay, or, if you like, the interpenetration, the interfusion of the emergent national idea on the one hand, and on the other hand an impulse clearly orientated towards that which the Consciousness Soul seeks to realize. And for reasons that we shall see later, it is precisely because of these events that the impulse of the Consciousness Soul breaks through in England and assumes the character of that national impulse; hence its peculiarly English flavour or nuance. We have now considered many of the factors which shaped Europe at the beginning of the age of the Consciousness Soul.

Behind all this, concealed as it were in the background, a virtual enigma to Europe, we see developing the later configuration of Russia, rightly regarded as an unknown quantity because it bears within it the seeds of the future. But first of all it is born of tradition, or, at least, of that which does not come from the Consciousness Soul and certainly not from the human soul. . . . None of the three elements which helped to fashion the configuration of Russia originated in the Russian soul. The first was the heritage of Byzantium, of Byzantine Catholicism; the second was that which had streamed in through the mingling of Nordic and Slav blood; the third was that which was transmitted by Asia. None of these three elements was the creation of the Russian soul; but it was these elements which moulded that strange, enigmatic structure which developed in the East and was concealed from the happenings in Europe.

Let us now try to find the common characteristic of all these things, of all these symptoms. They have one common

## Lecture I

characteristic which is very striking. We need only compare the real driving forces in human evolution today with those of former times and we perceive a significant difference which will indicate to us the quintessential character of the culture of the Consciousness Soul and that of the Rational and Intellectual Soul.

In order to see this situation in clearer perspective we can compare it with the impulse of Christianity which in every man must spring from the inmost depths of his being, an impulse which passes over into the events of history, but which springs from man's inner life. In the evolution of the earth Christianity is the most powerful impulse of this nature. We can, of course, consider impulses of lesser import, for example, those which influenced Roman civilization throughout the Augustan age, or we need only glance at the rich efflorescence of the Greek soul. We see everywhere new creative impulses entering into the evolution of mankind. In this respect, however, our present epoch brings to birth nothing new; at best we can speak of a rebirth, a revival of the past, for all the impulses which are operative here no longer spring from the human soul. The first thing that strikes us is the national idea, as it is often called—more correctly one should speak of the national impulse. It is not a creation of the individual soul, but is rooted in what we have received from inheritance, in what is already established. What emerges from the manifold spiritual impulses of Hellenism is something totally different. This national impulse is a rightful claim to something which is already present like a product of nature. As member of a national group man creates nothing of himself; he merely underlines the fact that, in a certain sense, he has developed naturally like a plant, like a member of the natural order. I intentionally called your attention earlier on to the fact that Asia's contribution to Europe (and only its external aspect was perceptible to

## From Symptom to Reality in Modern History

European culture) was something natural and spontaneous. The irruption of the Mongols, and later of the Osmanlis[8] into Europe, though their influence was considerable, did not lead to any creative impulse in Europe. Russia too produced no creative impulse, nothing that was particularly characteristic of the Russian soul. This was the work solely of the Byzantine and Asiatic element, this mixture of Nordic and Slav blood. In these peoples it is given facts, facts of nature which determine the lives of men—nothing in reality is created by the human soul. Let us bear this in mind, for it will serve as a point of departure for what is to follow. From the fifteenth century on the demands of mankind are of a totally different character.

Hitherto we have considered the external facts of history; let us now turn to the more inward happenings which are related more to the impulse of the Consciousness Soul which is breaking through the shell of the human soul. Let us consider, for example, the Council of Constance[9] and the burning of Hus. In Hus we see a personality who stands out, so to speak, like a human volcano. The Council of Constance which passed sentence on him opened in 1414, in the early years of the fifteenth century which marked the birth of the Consciousness Soul. Now in the annals of modern history Hus stands out as a symbol of protest against the suggestionism of the universalist impulse of Catholicism. In Jan Hus the Consciousness Soul itself rebels against all that the Rational or Intellectual soul had received from this universalist Catholic impulse. And this was not an isolated phenomenon—we could show how this ground had already been prepared by the struggle of the Albigenses against Catholic domination. In Savanarola in Italy and in others we see the revolt of the autonomous personality who wishes to arrive at his religious faith by relying upon his own judgement and rejects the suggestionism of papal Catholicism.

## Lecture I

And this same spirit of independence persists in Luther, in the emancipation of the Anglican Church from Rome (an extremely interesting and significant phenomenon), and in the Calvinist influence in certain regions of Europe. It is like a wave that sweeps over the whole of civilized Europe; it is an expression of the inner life, something more inward than the other influences, something which is already more closely linked with the soul of man, but in a different way from before.

After all, what do we admire in Calvin, in Luther when we consider them as historical figures? What do we admire in those who liberated the Anglican Church from Roman Catholic tutelage?—Not new creative ideas, not fresh spiritual insights, but the energy with which they endeavoured to pour traditional ideas into a new mould. Whereas these traditional ideas had formerly been accepted by the Rational or Intellectual Soul which was more instinctive or less conscious, they had now to be accepted by the Consciousness Soul which is autonomous. But this did not lead to the birth of new ideas, a new confession of faith. Time-honoured ideas are called in question, but no new symbol is found to replace them. The further we look back into the past—just think of the wealth of symbols created by man! Truly, a symbol such as the symbol of the Eucharist had to be created one day by the soul of man. In the age of Luther and Calvin there were endless disputes over the Eucharist as to whether it should be administered in both kinds or in one kind! But an autonomous impulse, an individual creation of the human soul was nowhere to be found. The dawning of the Consciousness Soul signifies a new relationship to these problems but does not herald the birth of new impulses.

When this new epoch dawns the budding Consciousness Soul is operative in it and manifests itself in historical symptoms. On the one hand we see the national impulses at work, on the other hand we see, striking at the very roots of religious faith, the revolt of the personality that strives for autonomy because the Consciousness Soul seeks to burst its bonds. And we must study the effects of these two forces when we consider the further development of the two representative national states, France and England. These forces gather strength, but are clearly differentiated and show how the two impulses, that of nationalism and that of personality, react upon each other differently in France and England. They create nothing new, but show the traditional past under new forms as the basis for the historical structure of Europe. This reinforcement of the national impulse is particularly evident in England where the personal element that in Hus, for example, assumed the form of religious pathos, unites with the national element, and the impulse of personality, of the Consciousness Soul, increasingly paves the way for parliamentary government, so that in England everything takes on a political aspect. In France—by contrast —despite the national element that exercises a powerful influence by reason of the native temperament and other things—the independence, the autonomy of the personality predominates and gives another nuance. Whilst England lays greater emphasis upon the national element, in France the active tendency is visibly more towards the element of personality. One must make a close study of these things.

That these forces act objectively—they are in no way connected with the arbitrary actions of man—can be seen in the case where the one impulse is operative, but bears no fruit; it remains sterile because it finds no external support and because the counter-impulse is still sufficiently powerful to neutralize it. In France the national impulse had such a powerful impact that it was able to liberate the French people from the authority of the Pope and this explains why it was France that compelled the Pope to reside at Avignon

## Lecture I

and why in France the ground was prepared for the emancipation of the personality. In England too the national impulse exercised a powerful influence, but at the same time, as a natural inheritance, the impulse of personality was equally strong. In the field of culture the whole nation was to a large extent free from Roman influence and developed its own doctrinal structure. In Spain the same impulse was at work but could neither penetrate the existing national element, nor, like the personality, overcome the power of suggestionism. Here everything remained in an embryonic state and became decadent before it had time to develop.

External events, what are usually called historical facts, are in reality only symptoms. This is obvious after a moment's reflection. In 1476 an important battle was fought on Swiss soil. The defeat of Charles the Bold in the battle of Murten was an extremely significant symptom, for it gave the death blow to chivalry that was closely associated with the Papacy. In the battle of Murten we see a trend that was already spreading through the whole of civilized Europe at that time, a trend that to some extent only came to light in a typically representative phenomenon (i.e. the battle of Murten).

When a phenomenon of this nature emerges on the surface it meets with counter-pressure from the past. The normal course of evolution, as you know, is always accompanied by Luciferic and Ahrimanic forces which derive from backward impulses and seek to assert themselves. Every normal impulse entering into mankind must fight against the subtle invasion of Luciferic and Ahrimanic forces. Thus the impulse that was clearly manifest in Hus, Luther, Calvin and Wyclif had to battle with these forces. A symptom of this struggle is seen in the revolt of the United Netherlands and in the Luciferic-Ahrimanic personality of Philip of Spain. And one of the most significant turning points of modern times was the defeat of the Spanish Armada in 1588. With this

*From Symptom to Reality in Modern History*

defeat those forces which, emanating from Spain, had offered the strongest resistance to the emancipation of the personality were finally eliminated. The Dutch wars of independence and the defeat of the Armada are external symptoms and nothing more. In order to arrive at the underlying reality we must be prepared to probe beneath the surface, for when these 'waves' are thrown up we are the better able to see the inner reality of events. The wave of 1588, when the Armada was defeated, illustrates how the personality which, in the process of emancipation, seeks to develop within itself the Consciousness Soul, rose in revolt against the petrified forms inherited from the Rational or Intellectual soul.

It is absurd to regard historical evolution as a temporal series of causes and effects, the present as the consequence of the past, cause—effect, cause—effect, etcetera. That is extremely convenient, especially when one takes the academic approach to historical research. It is so very convenient—simply to stagger along step by step from one historical fact to the next. But if one is not blind or asleep, if one looks at things with an open mind, the historical symptoms themselves show how absurd such an approach is.

Let us take an historical symptom which is most illuminating from a certain point of view. All the new developments from the fifteenth century onwards which are characterized by the impulses I have already indicated—the rise of nationalism, the awakening of personality—all this evoked conflicts and antagonisms which led to the Thirty Years' War. The account of this war as presented by history is seldom dealt with from the standpoint of symptomatology. It can hardly be treated after the fashion of café chatter. After all it was of little importance for the destiny of Europe that Martinitz, Slavata and Fabricius[10] were thrown out of the window of the royal palace in Prague and would have been killed had there not been a dungheap beneath the

*Lecture I*

window which saved the lives of the emperor's emissaries. In reality the dungheap is supposed to have consisted of scraps of paper that the servants of the Hradschin had thrown out of the window and had left lying there until they finally formed a pile of rubbish. This anecdote provides a pleasant topic for café chatter, but one cannot pretend that it has any bearing on the evolution of mankind!

When we begin to study the Thirty Years' War—I need hardly remind you that it began in 1618—it is important to bear in mind that the cause of the war lies solely in confessional differences, in what had developed in opposition to the old Catholicism, to the old Catholic impulses. Everywhere serious conflicts had arisen through this antagonism between the recent development of personality and the suggestionism of the old Catholicism. When the conflict was brought to an end by the Peace of Westphalia in 1648[11] we ask ourselves the question: how did matters stand in 1648 in respect of this conflict between Protestantism and Catholicism? What had come of it? What changes had taken place in the course of thirty years? Nothing strikes us more forcbily than the fact that in this conflict between Catholicism and Protestantism and in everthing connected with it the situation in 1648 was exactly the same as it had been in 1618. Though, meanwhile, certain issues which had been the source of discord had been modified somewhat, the situation in Central Europe had remained unchanged since the outbreak of hostilities. But the intervention of foreign powers which was in no way connected with the causes of the conflict of 1618, this intervention, after the powers had found scope for their activity, gave a totally different complexion to the political forces in Europe. The political horizon of those who had been involved in the war was completely transformed. But the results of the peace of Westphalia, the changed situation in relation to the past, this had nothing whatsoever to do with the causes of the conflict in 1618.

This fact is extremely important, especially in the case of the Thirty Years' War, and illustrates how absurd it is to consider history, as is the usual practice, in terms of cause and effect. However, the consequence of these developments was that England and France owed their leading position in Europe to the outcome of this war. But their supremacy was in no way connected with the causes which provoked the war. And a most important factor in the march of modern history is this: following upon the Thirty Years' War the national impulses, in conjunction with the other impulses which I have described elsewhere, develop in such a way that France and England become the representative national states. There is much talk at the present time of the national principle in the East; but we must not forget that this principle passed from the West to the East. Like the trade winds, the national impulse flowed from West to East and we must bear this clearly in mind.

Now it is interesting to see how the same impulse—the national impulse in conjunction with the emancipation of the personality—assumes a totally different form in the two countries, where, as we saw, they began to be clearly differentiated in 1429. In France the emancipation of the personality within the national group develops in such a way that it turns inward. That is to say, if the national element is represented by the red line in the diagram below and on the one side of the line is the individual human being, and on the other side mankind, then in France the development of the national impulse is orientated towards man, towards the individual, in England towards mankind. France modifies the national element within the nation state in such a way that the national element tends to transform the inner being of man, to make him other than he is. In

*Lecture I*

England the personal element transcends nationalism and seeks to embrace the whole world and to promote everywhere the development of the personality. The Frenchman wishes rather to develop the personal element in the soul, the Englishman to extend the principle of personality to the whole of mankind. Here we see two entirely different trends—in both cases the basis is the national element. In the one case the national impulse turns inwards, towards the individual soul; in the other it is directed outwards,

*Mankind*

*red*

*Man*

towards the soul of mankind. In England and France therefore we have two parallel streams with two sharply contrasting tendencies. Only in France therefore, where the inner life of the personality was deeply influenced, could the political and social configuration which developed as I have described lead to the Revolution—via Louis XIV, etcetera. In England the national impulse led to a sober liberalism, because here it expressed itself externally, whilst in France it expressed itself inwardly, in the inner life of man.

This phenomenon, strangely enough, manifests itself also geographically, especially when we consider another turning point in modern history as symptom—the defeat of Napoleon, who was a product of the French Revolution, by the English at the battle of Trafalgar in 1805. What is revealed to us here? Napoleon, a strange representative it is true, but nonetheless a representative of the French make-up, signifies the withdrawal inwards—and geographically too, the withdrawal to the continent of Europe. If the following diagram represents Europe—Napoleon, precisely as a consequence of the battle of Trafalgar, is thrust back towards Europe (see arrow) and England is thrust outwards towards the whole world in the opposite direction. At the same time let us not forget that these two tendencies have

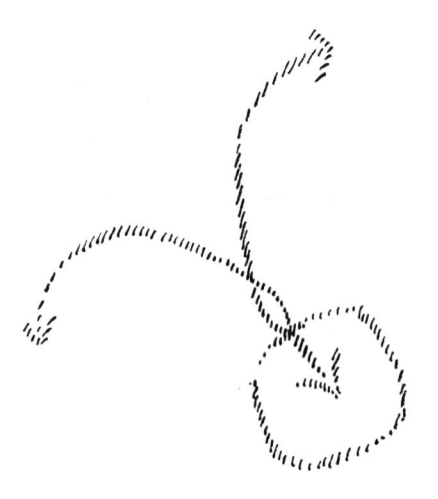

need of conflict, they must try conclusions with each other. And this is what happened in the struggle for supremacy in North America, which in some respects is a consequence of this turning point in 1805. Looking back a few decades before this date we see how the specifically French nuance, Romanism, is ousted in the interests of the world by the Anglo-Saxon element in North America.

Thus you can sense, if you really wish to, the forces which are at work here; like the magician's apprentice the impulse of the Consciousness Soul conjures up national impulses which implant themselves in mankind in divers forms

*Lecture I*

and with different nuances. We can only understand these things if we study the impulse of the Consciousness Soul in all its aspects, avoiding all prejudice and keeping our eyes open for what is important and what is unimportant and also for what is more or less characteristic so that from our observation of external symptoms we can then penetrate to the inner pattern of reality. For external appearances often belie the inner impulse of the personality, especially in an epoch when the personality is self-dependent. And this, too, becomes apparent when we study symptomatically the development of modern history. What is taught as history in our schools is quite unreal. The real facts are as follows: here is the surface movement of the water, here is the current (shaded red in the diagram.)

Now there are times when there breaks through into historical events—like the waves thrown up here, sometimes with the violence of a volcanic eruption—what lies beneath the surface. At other times, events emerge on the surface, and isolated historical events betray what lies beneath the surface. As symptoms they are especially characteristic. But sometimes there are symptoms where one must totally ignore external appearances when looking at the symptomatic fact.

Now there is a personality who is especially characteristic

## From Symptom to Reality in Modern History

of the emergence of the impulse of the Consciousness Soul in Western Europe, both on account of his personal development and on account of the place he occupies in contemporary history. At the beginning of the seventeenth century he was involved in this differentiation between the French impulse and the English impulse, a differentiation that had exercised a widespread influence upon the rest of Europe. In the seventeenth century this differentiation had been effective for some time and had become more pronounced. The personality who appeared on the stage of history at this time was a strange individual, whom we can depict in the following way: one could say that he was extremely generous, filled with deep and genuine gratitude for the knowledge imparted to him, infinitely grateful, in fact a model of gratitude for the kindness men showed towards him. He was a scholar who combined in his person almost the entire erudition of his day, a personality who was extremely peace-loving, a sovereign indifferent to the intrigues of the world, wholly devoted to the ideal of universal peace, extremely prudent in decisions and resolutions, and most kindly disposed towards his fellow men. Such is the portrait that one could sketch of this personality. If one takes a partial view, it is possible to portray him in this way and this is the external view that history presents.

It is also possible to portray him from another angle which is equally partial. One could say that he was an outrageous spendthrift without the slightest notion of his financial resources, a pedant, a typical professor whose erudition was shot through with abstractions and pedantry. Or one could say that he was timid and irresolute, and whenever called upon to defend some principle he would evade the issue out of pusillanimity, preferring peace at any price. It could also be said of him that he was shrewd or crafty and wormed his way through life by artfully choosing the path that always

## Lecture I

guaranteed success. Or that he endeavoured to establish relationships with others as children are wont to do. His friendships betrayed a frankly childish element which, in his veneration for others and in the adulation others accorded him, was transformed into romantic infatuation. One can adopt either of these points of view. And in fact there were some who described him from the one angle, others from the other angle, and many from both angles. Such was the historical personality of James I[12] who reigned from 1603 to 1625. Whichever point of view we take, in both cases the cap fits perfectly. In neither case do we know what he really felt or thought as a typical representative of contemporary evolution. And yet, precisely in the epoch when James I was King of England a hidden current rises to the surface and the symptoms manifested at that time are characteristic of the underlying reality. We will speak more of this tomorrow.

## LECTURE II

Yesterday I attempted to sketch in broad outline the symptoms of the recent historical evolution of mankind and finally included in this complex of symptoms—at first not pursuing this in greater detail, for we shall have time for that later on, but confining ourselves more to the general characteristics—the strange figure of James I, King of England, at the beginning of the seventeenth century. This enigmatic figure appeared on the stage of history midway between the beginning of the fifth post-Atlantean epoch and the nineteenth century, a century that was important and decisive. It is not my task today—we can discuss this later—to speak of the many mysteries associated with the personality of James I. I must, however, draw your attention to the strange part, strange in a symptomatic manner, which James I plays in contemporary history. He was a man who was a bundle of contradictions and yesterday I attempted to show two contradictory aspects of his character. One can point to his virtues or his defects, according to one's point of view.

James's whole environment, the framework of the political and social conditions which developed out of the conditions I have described to you—his reign which saw the emergence of the idea of the state born of the national impulse and witnessed the rise of the parliamentary system of government or at least of a democratic system tending towards liberal ideas—this world was wholly alien to him, it was a world in which he was never really at home. If we look a little more closely at what characterizes the entire post-Atlantean epoch from the point of view of the birth of the Consciousness

## Lecture II

Soul, we shall have a clearer understanding of James I. We then see him as a personality who exhibits that radical contradiction that we so easily associate with personalities of the era of the Consciousness Soul. In the epoch of the Consciousness Soul the personality lost the value it owed in former times to the instinctive life, because it had not yet fully developed self-awareness. In earlier epochs the personality expressed itself with elemental force—and I hope I shall not be misunderstood if I say this—with brute force, with an animal force that was nonetheless endowed with soul and human attributes. The personality expressed itself instinctively, it had not yet emerged from the group soul. And now it had to break free, to become self-sufficient and stand on its own feet. Consequently the personality was faced with a strange and paradoxical situation. On the one hand, everything that had formerly existed for the purposes of personal satisfaction was sloughed off, the instincts were blunted and henceforth the soul had gradually to become the seat of the personality. In brief, the soul had to take full command.

That a contradiction exists is evident from what I said yesterday. Whereas in earlier times, when the personality had not developed self-consciousness, men had been creative and had assimilated the creative forces of their culture, these creative energies were now exhausted and the soul had become sterile. And yet the soul occupies the central place in man's being; for the essence of the personal element is that the self-sufficient soul becomes the focal point of man's being. Consequently great personalities of antiquity such as Augustus, Julius Caesar, Pericles—and I could mention many others—will never be seen again. The dynamic, elemental energy of the personality declines and there emerges what is later called the democratic outlook which, with its egalitarian doctrine, standardizes the personality. And it is

*From Symptom to Reality in Modern History*

precisely in this egalitarian process that the personality seeks to manifest itself—truly a radical contradiction!

Now everyone's station in life is determined by his Karma. It was the karmic destiny of James I to occupy the throne. In the epoch of the Persian Kings, of the Mongol Khans and even in the century when the Pope crowned the Magyar Istwan I[1] with the sacred crown of St. Stephen, the personality counted for something in a position of authority, he regarded himself as the natural heir to his position. In the position he occupied, even in his position as Sovereign, James I resembled a man dressed in an ill-fitting garment. One could say that in relation to the duties and responsibilities that devolved upon him he was, in every respect, like a man dressed in a garment that ill became him. As a child he had been brought up as a Calvinist; later he was converted to Anglicanism, but fundamentally he was indifferent to both confessions. In his heart of hearts he felt all this to be a masquerade which was foreign to him. He was called upon to rule as sovereign in the coming age of parliamentary liberalism which had already been in existence for some time. In conversation with others he was intelligent and shrewd, but nobody really understood what he wanted because all the others wanted something different. He came of an old Catholic family, the Stuarts. But when he ascended the throne of England the Catholics were the first to realize that they had nothing to hope for from him. In 1605 a group of Catholics drew up plans to blow up the Houses of Parliament when the King and his chief ministers were present. They planted twenty barrels of gunpowder in the cellar beneath the parliamentary building. This was the famous Gunpowder Plot. The conspiracy failed because a Catholic fellow-conspirator betrayed the plot, otherwise James I would have been blown up together with his parliament. James I was a misfit because he was a personality, and the

## Lecture II

personality has something singular, something unusual in its make-up. It is characterized by a certain detachment, a certain self-sufficiency. But in the era of the personality everyone wishes to be a personality and that is the inherent contradiction of this epoch. We must always bear this in mind. It is not that one rejects the idea of king or pope; it is not a question of suppressing these offices, but simply that if a king or a pope already exists, everyone would like to be pope, everyone would like to be king. Thus papacy, royalty and democracy would be realized at the same time. All these things come to mind when we consider the symptom typified by this strange personality, James I. He was in every respect a man of the new age and was involved in this age with all the contradictions latent in the personality. As I mentioned yesterday those who characterized him from the one angle were mistaken, and those who characterized from the other angle were equally mistaken; and the picture of him which we derive from his writings is also misleading. For even what he himself wrote does not give us any clear insight into his soul. Thus, if we do not consider him from an esoteric point of view he remains a great enigma on the threshold of the seventeenth century, occupying a position which, from a certain point of view, revealed in the most radical fashion the dawn of the impulse of modern times.

I spoke yesterday of the developments in Western Europe and of the difference between the French and English character. This differentiation began to show itself in the fifteenth century, and this turning point was signalized by the appearance of Joan of Arc in 1429. And we saw how, in England, the emancipation of the personality was associated with the aspiration to extend the principle of the personality to the whole world, how in France the emancipation of the personality—in both countries originating in the national idea—was associated with the aspiration to lay hold of the inner life as far as possible and to make it autonomous. This was the situation in which James I found himself at the beginning of the seventeenth century, a personality who typified all the contradictions inherent in the personal element. In characterizing symptoms one must never seek to be over scrupulously explicit, one must always leave room for something unexplained, otherwise one makes no headway. And this is why I prefer not to provide you with a neatly finished portrait of James I, but to leave something to the imagination, something to reflect upon.

A radical difference between the English and French make-up became increasingly evident. Out of the chaos of the Thirty Years' War there developed in France an increasing emphasis upon what may be called the idea of the state. If one wishes to study the consolidation of the state idea one need only take the example, though the example is somewhat unusual, of the French national state and its rise to power and splendour under Louis XIV and its subsequent decline. We see how within this national state the first shoots then develop into that widespread emancipation of the personality which is the legacy of the French Revolution.

The French Revolution brought to the fore three impulses of human life which are fully justified—the desire for fraternity, liberty and equality. But I have already indicated on another occasion* how, within the framework of the French Revolution, this triad, fraternity, liberty and equality, conflicted with the genuine evolution of mankind. When dealing with the evolution of mankind one cannot speak of fraternity, liberty and equality without relating them in some way to the tripartite division of man. In relation to the community life at the physical level mankind must gradually

* In the lecture of 18th October, 1916 in *Inner Entwicklungsimpulse der Menschheit* (Bibl. Nr. 171).

## Lecture II

develop fraternity in the epoch of the Consciousness Soul. It would be the greatest misfortune and a sign of regression in evolution if, at the close of the fifth post-Atlantean epoch, the epoch of the Consciousness Soul, mankind had not developed fraternity at least to a large extent. But we can only fully understand fraternity if we think of it in connection with community life, the physical bond between man and man. Only at the level of the psychic life is it possible to speak of liberty. It would be a mistake to imagine that liberty can be realized in the external, corporeal life of the community; liberty, however, can be realized between individuals at the psychic level. One must not envisage man as a hybrid unity and then speak of fraternity, liberty and equality. We must realize that man is divided into body, soul and spirit, that men only attain to liberty when they seek to become inwardly free, free in their soul life, and can only be equal in relation to the spirit. That which lays hold of us spiritually is the same for all. Men strive for the spirit because the fifth post-Atlantean epoch, the era of the Consciousness Soul, strives for the Spirit Self. And in this aspiration to the spirit all men are equal, just as in death all men are equal, as the popular adage says. But if one does not apportion fraternity, liberty and equality rightly amongst these three different vehicles of man, but simply assigns them indiscriminately, saying: man shall live fraternally on earth, he shall be free and equal—then only confusion results.

Considered as a symptom, the French Revolution is extraordinarily interesting. It presents—in the form of slogans applied haphazardly and indiscriminately to the whole human being—that which must gradually be developed in the course of the epoch of the Consciousness Soul, from 1413 to the year 3573, with all the spiritual resources at man's disposal. The task of this epoch is to achieve fraternity on the physical plane, liberty on the psychic plane and equality on the spiritual plane. But without any understanding of this relationship, confusing everything indiscriminately, this quintessence of the fifth post-Atlantean epoch appears in the French Revolution in the form of slogans. The soul of this epoch is comprised in three words (fraternity, liberty and equality), but they are not understood. It is unable therefore at first to find social embodiment and this leads to untold confusion. It cannot find any external social embodiment, but significantly, is present as the 'demanding soul', a soul in search of embodiment. All the inner soul life which must inform this fifth post-Atlantean epoch remains uncomprehended and cannot find any means of expression. And here we are confronted with a symptom of immense importance.

When that which is to be realized in the course of the coming epoch manifests itself almost violently at first, we are far removed from that state of equilibrium which man needs for his development, far removed from those forces which are innate in men through their connection with their own particular hierarchies. The beam of the balance dips sharply to one side. In the interplay between the Luciferic and Ahrimanic influences it dips sharply to the side of Lucifer as a result of the French Revolution. This provokes a reaction. I am here speaking more than figuratively, I am speaking *imaginatively*. You must not read too much into the words; above all you must not take them literally. In what appeared in the French Revolution we see, to some extent, the soul of the fifth post-Atlantean epoch without social embodiment, without corporeal existence. It is abstract, purely emotional, a soul in search of embodiment ... and this can only be realized in the course of millennia, or at least in the course of centuries. But because in the course of evolution the balance inclines to one side, it provokes a

## Lecture II

reaction and swings to the other pole. In the French Revolution everything is in a state of ferment, everything runs counter to the rhythm of human evolution. Because the balance inclines to the opposite pole a situation now arises where everything (no longer in a state of equilibrium, but alternating between the Luciferic and Ahrimanic poles) is once again fully in accordance with the human rhythm, with the impersonal claims of the personality. In Napoleon there appears subsequently a figure who is fashioned entirely in conformity with the rhythm of the personality, but with a tendency to the opposite pole. Seven years of sovereignty, fourteen years of imperial splendour and harassment of Europe, the years of his ascent to power, then seven years of decline, the first years of which he spent once again in disrupting the peace of Europe—all in accordance with a strict rhythm: seven years, then twice seven years and then again seven years, a rhythm of septennia.

I have been at great pains (and I have alluded to this on various occasions) to trace the soul of Napoleon. It is possible, as you know, to undertake these studies of the human soul in divers ways by means of spiritual scientific investigation. And you will recall no doubt how investigations were undertaken to discover the previous incarnations of Novalis.[2] I have been at great pains to follow the destiny of Napoleon's soul in its journey after his death. I have been unable to find it and do not think I shall ever be able to find it, for it is probably not to be found. And this no doubt accounts for the enigma of Napoleon's life that unfolds with clockwork precision in seven-year rhythms. We can best understand this soul if we regard it as the complete antithesis of a soul such as that of James I, or again as the antithesis of the abstraction of the French Revolution: the Revolution all soul without body, Napoleon all body without soul, but a body compounded of all the contradictions of the age. In this strange juxtaposition of the Revolution and Napoleon lies one of the greatest enigmas of contemporary evolution. One has the impression that a soul wanted to incarnate in the world, appeared without a body, clamoured for incarnation amongst the revolutionaries of the eighteenth century, but was unable to find a body ... and that only externally a body offered itself, a body which for its part could not find a soul, i.e. Napoleon. In these things there are more than merely ingenious allusions or characterizations, they harbour important impulses of historical development. They must of course be regarded as symptoms. Here, amongst ourselves, I use the terminology of spiritual science. But what I have just said could equally well be said anywhere if clothed in slightly different terminology.

When we attempt to pursue further the symptomatology of recent times we see the English character unfolding in successive stages in relative peace. Up to the end of the nineteenth century it developed fairly uniformly, it shaped the ideal of liberalism in relative peace. The development of the French character was more tempestuous, so much so that when we follow the thread of events in the history of France in the nineteenth century we never really know how a later event came to be associated with the previous event; they seem to follow each other without motivation so to speak. The major feature of the historical development of France in the nineteenth century is this absence of motivation. No reproach is implied here—I am speaking quite dispassionately. I merely wish to characterize.

We shall never be able to understand the whole symptom-complex of contemporary history if we do not perceive, as I mentioned yesterday, that in everything that takes place, both on the external plane or on the plane of the inner life, something else to be at work which I would like to characterize as follows. Even before the dawn of the fifth post-

## Lecture II

Atlantean epoch, the epoch of the Consciousness Soul, one already sensed its approach. Certain sensitives had a prophetic intimation of its advent and they felt its true character. They felt that the epoch was approaching when the personality was destined to emancipate itself, that in a certain respect it would be an unproductive era, an era without creative energy, that especially in the cultural field which fertilizes both the historical and the social life, it would be compelled to live on the legacy of the past.

This is the real motive behind the Crusades which preceded the epoch of the Consciousness Soul. Why did the people of Europe take up arms in order to recover the Holy Land and the city of Jerusalem with the Holy Sepulchre? Because they were neither able, nor willing, in the era of the Consciousness Soul, to search for a new mission, for an idea that was new and original; they endeavoured to recover the true form and substance of the ancient traditions. 'To Jerusalem' was the watchword—in order to rediscover the past and incorporate it in evolution in a form different from that of Rome. People sensed that the Crusades marked the dawn of the era of the Consciousness Soul with its characteristic sterility. And it was in connection with the Crusades that there was founded the Order of the Templars* which was suppressed by Philip the Fair. With this Order the oriental mysteries were introduced into Europe and left their impress on European culture. It is true that Philip the Fair had the members of the Order executed as heretics and their wealth confiscated,† but the Templar impulses had penetrated into European life through various channels and continued to exercise an influence through the medium of numerous occult lodges which then began to work exoteric-

\* See note 3 to Lecture I.
† Also discussed in *Kosmische und menschliche Geschichte* Vol III, Lecture VI; Vol IV, Lecture I.

ally and so gradually built up opposition to Rome. On the one side stood Rome, alone at first; then she allied herself with the Jesuits. On the other side was ranged—closely connected with the Christian element and completely alien to Rome—everything that of necessity had to stand in opposition to Rome and which even Rome felt, and still feels, to be a powerful body of opposition. How is one to account for the fact that, in the face of what I described yesterday as the suggestive power of this universalist impulse which emanated from Rome, people in the West came to accept and adopt gnostic teachings, ideas, symbols and rites which were of oriental provenance? What was the deeper underlying impulse behind this phenomenon? If we look into this question we shall be able to discover the real motive behind it.

The Consciousness Soul was destined to emerge. As a bulwark against the Consciousness Soul Rome wished to preserve, and still preserves today, a culture based on suggestionism, a culture that is calculated to arrest man's progress towards the development of the Consciousness Soul and keep him at the level of the Rational or Intellectual Soul. This is the real battle which Rome wages against the tide of progress. Rome wishes to cling to an outlook which is valid for the Rational Soul at a time when mankind seeks to progress towards the development of the Consciousness Soul.

On the other hand, in progressing towards the Consciousness Soul mankind in effect finds itself in a most unhappy position which for the vast majority of people during the first centuries of the era of the Consciousness Soul and up to our own time was felt at first to be rather disturbing. The epoch of the Consciousness Soul demands that man should stand on his own feet, be self-sufficient and, as personality, emancipate himself. He must abandon the old supports. He

## Lecture II

can no longer allow himself to be persuaded into what he should believe; he must work out for himself his own religious faith. This was felt to be a dangerous precedent. When the epoch of the Consciousness Soul dawned it was instinctively felt that man was losing his former centre of gravity ... and must find a new one. But on the other hand if he remains passive, what are the possibilities before him? One possibility is simply to give him a free hand in his search for the Consciousness Soul, to set him free to develop in his own way. A second possibility is that, if left to himself, Rome then assumes great importance and may exercise considerable influence upon him, if it should succeed in curbing his efforts to develop the Consciousness Soul in order to keep him at the stage of the Rational Soul. And the consequence of that would be that man could attain neither to the Consciousness Soul nor to the Spirit Self and would therefore sacrifice his possibility of future development. This would be only one of the paths by which future evolution might be imperilled.

A third possibility is to proceed in a still more radical fashion. In order that man may not be caught between the striving for the Consciousness Soul and the limitations of consciousness imposed upon him by Rome, attempts were made to stifle his aspiration for the Consciousness Soul, to undermine this aspiration even more radically than Rome. This is achieved by emasculating the progressive impulses and substituting for their dynamism the dead hand of tradition which had been brought over from the East, though originally the Templars, who had been esoterically initiated, had had a different object in view. But after the leaders had been massacred, after the suppression of the Templar Order by Philip the Fair, something of this culture which had been brought over from the East survived, not amongst isolated individuals, but in the field of history. What the

Templars had brought over gradually infiltrated into Europe through numerous channels (as I have already indicated), but to a large extent was divested of its spiritual substance. What the Templars transmitted was, in the main, the substance of the third post-Atlantean epoch . . . Catholicism transmitted the substance of the fourth epoch. And that from which spiritual substance had been extracted like the juice from a lemon, that which was transmitted in the form of exoteric freemasonry in the York and Scottish lodges and pervaded especially the false esotericism of the English speaking peoples—this squeezed out lemon which contained the secrets of the Egypto-Chaldaean epoch, the third post-Atlantean epoch, now served as a means of implanting desiccated impulses into the life of the Consciousness Soul.

Thus there arises a situation which is a travesty of the future course of evolution. Recall for a moment what I said to you on a former occasion\* when speaking of the seven epochs of evolution. We start from the Atlantean catastrophe; then follow the post-Atlantean epochs with their corresponding relationships. $1 = 7$, $2 = 6$, $3 = 5$, 4. The fourth epoch constitutes the centre without any corresponding relationship. The characteristics of the third epoch are repeated at a higher level in the fifth epoch, those of the second epoch at a higher level in the sixth epoch and those of the old Indian epoch reappear in the seventh epoch. These overlapping correlations occur in history. Isolated individuals were conscious of this. For example, when Kepler attempted in the fifth post-Atlantean epoch to explain after his own fashion the harmony of the Cosmos by his three laws saying, 'I offer you the golden vessels of the Egyptians . . .' etcetera—he was aware that in the man of the fifth post-Atlantean epoch there is a revival of

\* *The Spiritual Guidance of Man and Humanity*, Anthroposophic Press, 1970.

*Lecture II*

the substance of the third epoch. In a certain sense, when one takes over the esotericism, the rites of the Egypto-Chaldaean epoch, one creates a semblance of what is destined to be realized in the present epoch. But what one takes over from the past can be used not only to suppress the autonomy of the Consciousness Soul by the power of suggestion, but also to blunt, even to paralyse its dynamic energy. And in this respect a large measure of success has been achieved; the incipient Consciousness Soul has been anaesthetized to a large extent.

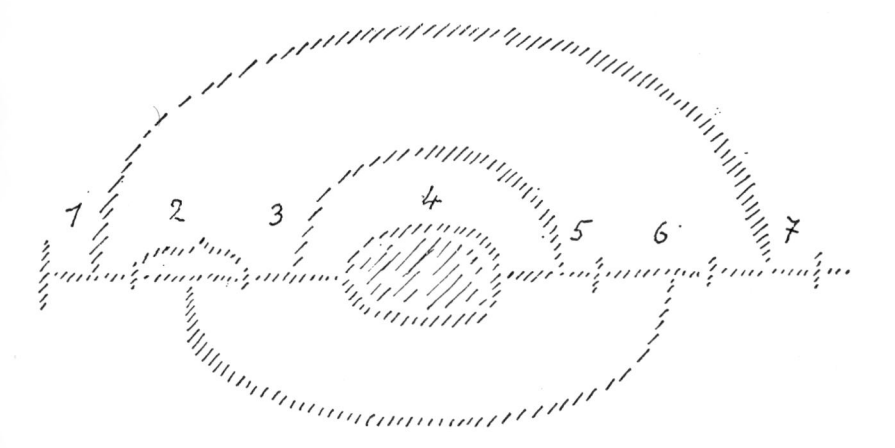

*1   2   3   4   5   6   7*

Rome—I am now speaking figuratively—makes use of incense and induces a condition of semi-consciousness by evoking a dreamlike state. But the movement to which I am now referring lulls people to sleep (i.e. the Consciousness Soul) completely. Moreover as history bears witness, this condition penetrated also into contemporary evolution. Thus on the one hand we have what is created through the tempestuous emergence of fraternity, liberty and equality, whilst on the other hand the impulse already exists which prevents mankind in the course of the fifth post-Atlantean epoch from perceiving clearly how fraternity, liberty and equality are to lay hold of man; for they can only perceive this clearly when they are able to make use of the Consciousness Soul in order to arrive at true self-knowledge, i.e. when they awake in the Consciousness Soul. And when men awake in the Consciousness Soul they become aware of themselves in the body, the soul and the spirit; and this is precisely what must be prevented. We have therefore two streams in contemporary history: on the one hand, since the impulse towards the Consciousness Soul already exists, there is the chaotic search for fraternity, liberty and equality. On the other hand we see the efforts on the part of widely differing Orders to suppress this awakening in the Consciousness Soul for their own ends. These two currents interact throughout the whole history of modern times.

Now as the new era bursts upon the eighteenth century and the early years of the nineteenth century, something new is being prepared. Up to the middle of the nineteenth century we see at first a powerful urge towards the emancipation of the personality because, when so many currents are active, the new development does not unfold gradually and smoothly, but ebbs and flows. And we see developing, on a basis of nationalism, and in response to the other impulses I have already mentioned in connection with the West of Europe, that which tends towards the emancipation of the personality, that which seeks to overcome nationality and to attain to the universal-human. But this impulse cannot really develop independently on account of the counter-impulse from those Orders which, especially in England, contaminate the whole of public life much more than people imagine. And so we see strange personalities appear, such as Richard Cobden and John Bright,[3] who were ardent advocates of the emancipation of the personality, of the triumph of the personality over nationalism the world over. They went so far as to touch upon

## Lecture II

something which could be of the greatest political significance if it should ever find its way into modern historical evolution! Differentiated according to the different countries, this principle of non-intervention in the affairs of others became the fundamental principle of English liberalism, and these two personalities of course defined it in terms of their own country. It was something of great significance, and scarcely had it been formulated before it was stifled by that other aspiration which stemmed from the impulse of the third post-Atlantean epoch. Thus up to the middle of the nineteenth century there emerged what is usually called liberalism, liberal opinion ... soon to be called free-thinking—according to one's taste. I am referring to that outlook which, in the political sphere, expressed itself most clearly in the eighteenth century in the form of political enlightenment, in the nineteenth as the struggle for political liberalism[4] which gradually lost momentum and died out in the last third of the century.

The liberal element which was still prevalent everywhere in the sixties gradually ceased to be a vital force in the life of the country and was replaced by something else. We now touch upon significant symptoms of recent history. For a time the impact of the Consciousness Soul was such that it threw up a wave of liberalism. But a flood tide is followed by an ebb tide (blue). And this ebb tide is the counter-thrust to liberalism (arrow pointing downwards). Let us look at this more closely. Liberalism was born of self-discipline; its representatives tried to free themselves from constraint. They cast off the fetters of narrow prejudice and conventional ideas; they cut their moorings, if I may use the nautical expression, and refused to allow their ship to be boarded. They were imbued with universal, human ideals, but socialism was active in the preparation of the new age and gradually attracted to itself these so-called liberal ideas which found so little support. By the middle of the nineteenth century there was no political future for liberal ideas, for their representatives in later years give more or less the impression of casualties of political thinking. The latter-day liberal parties were simply stragglers, for, after the middle of the nineteenth century, the effect of what emerged from the Orders and secret societies of the West began to make its influence increasingly felt, namely, the anaesthetization, the stifling of the Consciousness Soul. Under these circumstances spirit and soul are no longer active, and only the forces of the phenomenal or sensible world are operative. And so from the middle of the nineteenth century these forces manifested in the form of socialism of every kind, a socialism that was conscious of itself, of its power and importance.

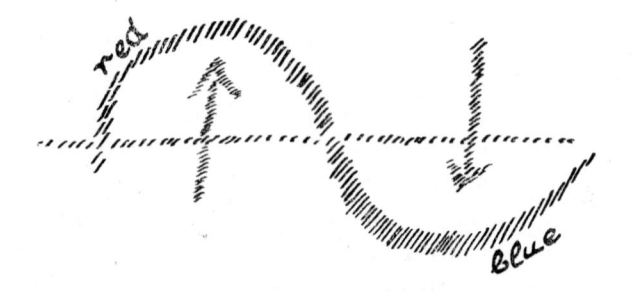

But this socialism is only possible if imbued with spirit, not with pseudo-spirit, with the mask of spirit, with mere rationalism that can only apprehend the inorganic, i.e. dead forms. It was with this 'dead' knowledge that Lassalle[5] first wrestled, but it was Marx and Engels who elaborated it. Thus, in socialism which endeavoured to translate theory into practice, and in practice was a total failure because it was too theoretical, there appeared one of the most important symptoms of the recent historical evolution of mankind.

## Lecture II

I now propose to examine a few characteristic features of this socialism.

Modern socialism is characterized by three tenets or three interrelated tenets—the materialist conception of history,[6] the theory of surplus value and the theory of the class struggle.[6] In the main these convictions are held by millions today. In order to have a clear understanding of these symptoms which will form the basis of our study tomorrow, let us first attempt to establish what we mean by the materialist conception of history.

The materialist conception of history believes that the course of evolution is determined by economic factors. Men must eat and drink, acquire the necessities of life from various sources. They must trade, exchange goods and produce what nature does not produce unaided without man's intervention. This constitutes the driving force of evolution. How is one to explain, for example, the appearance of men such as Lessing in the eighteenth century? Since the sixteenth century, and especially in the eighteenth century, the introduction of the mechanical loom and spinning-jenny has created a sharp division—and the first signs were already apparent—between the bourgeoisie and the rising proletariat. The proletariat hardly existed as yet, but it was already smouldering beneath the surface. In the course of recent economic development the bourgeoisie had gained in strength at the expense of the former estates. Through his mode of life which entailed the employment of labour, through his refusal to recognize the former estates, through his control over the production, distribution and manufacture of commodities, the bourgeois developed a certain way of thinking that was peculiar to his class and which was simply an ideological superstructure covering his methods of production, manufacture and distribution. And this determined his particular mode of thought. The peasant, by contrast, who is surrounded by nature and lives in communion with nature has a different outlook. But his way of thinking too is only an ideology. What matters is the way in which he produces and markets his merchandise. The middle classes have a different outlook from the peasant because they are crowded together in towns; they are urbanized, no longer bound to the soil, are indifferent to nature, and their relationship to nature is abstract and impersonal. The bourgeois becomes a rationalist and thinks of God in general and abstract terms. This is the consequence of his mercantile activity—an extreme view perhaps, but nonetheless it contains a grain of truth. Because of the way in which goods have been manufactured and marketed since the sixteenth century, a way of thinking developed which was reflected in a particular way in Lessing. He represents the bourgeoisie at its apogee, whilst the proletariat lags behind in its development. In the same way Herder and Goethe are explained as the products of their environment, by their bourgeois mentality which is merely a superstructure. To the purely materialist outlook only the fruits of economic activities, the production, manufacture and marketing of goods, are real.

Such is the materialist conception of history. It accounts for Christianity by showing how, at the beginning of our era, the conditions of commercial exchange between East and West had changed, how the exploitation of slaves and the relationship between masters and slaves had been modified and how then an ideological superstructure—Christianity—had been erected upon this play of economic interests. And because men were also under the necessity of producing what they ate and what they had to sell in order to provide for their sustenance in a different way from formerly, they developed in consequence a different way of thinking. And because a radical change occurred in the economic life at the beginning of our era, a radical change also occurred in

## Lecture II

the ideological superstructure which is characterized as Christianity. This is the first of those tenets which have found their way into the hearts of millions since the middle of the nineteenth century.

The entrenched bourgeoisie has no idea how firmly the materialist conception of history has taken hold of wide sections of the population. Of course the professors who expatiate on history, on the darker face of history, find a ready audience. But even amongst the professors a few have recently felt secretly drawn towards Marxism. But they have no following amongst the broad masses of the people. That is what we have come to in the epoch of the Consciousness Soul . . . meanwhile the impulse of the Consciousness Soul continues to operate. People are beginning to wake up in so far as they are permitted to do so. On the one hand attempts are made to lull them to sleep; on the other hand, however, they would like to wake from their sleep. Since they are familiar only with the purely phenomenal world they have developed a materialist conception of history. Here is the origin of those strange symptoms.

Schiller, one of the noblest and most liberal of minds, was greatly admired and for years homage was paid to his memory. In 1859 monuments were erected everywhere to commemorate the centenary of his birth. In my youth there lived in Vienna a man called Heinrich Deinhardt who, in a beautiful book, tried to introduce people to the fundamental ideas which Schiller expressed in his *Letters on the aesthetic education of man*. The entire edition was pulped. The author had the misfortune to be caught, I believe, by a passing tram. He fell down in the street and broke his leg. Although he suffered only a minor fracture it refused to heal because he was badly undernourished. He never recovered from the accident. That is only a symptom of the treatment reserved in the nineteenth century for those who sought to interpret

Schiller to the public, to awaken the consciousness of the time to the nobility of Schiller's ideas! Of course, you will say—others will say: do we not meet with noble aspirations in all spheres? Undoubtedly, and we will speak of them later, but for the most part they only lead into a blind alley.

Such is the first of the socialist tenets; the second is the theory of surplus value.[6] It can be summarized roughly as follows: as a result of the new method of production, the man who is employed in the production and manufacture of goods must sell his labour-power as a commodity like other commodities. Thus two classes are created—the entrepreneurs and the workers. The entrepreneurs are the capitalists who control the means of production—factories, machinery, everything concerned with the means of production. The other class, the workers, have only their labour-power to sell. And because the capitalist who owns or controls the means of production can purchase on the open market the labour-power of the worker, he is in a position to pay him a bare subsistence wage, to reduce to a minimum the remuneration for the commodity labour-power. But the commodity labour-power, when put to use, creates a greater value than its own value. The difference between the value of labour and its product, i.e. the surplus value, goes into the pocket of the capitalist. Such is the Marxist theory of surplus value and it has the support of millions. And this situation has arisen simply through the particular economic structure of the social life in recent times. Ultimately this leads to the class struggle, to exploiters and exploited.

Fundamentally these are the tenets which, since the middle of the nineteenth century, have increasingly won over limited circles at first, then political groups and parties, and finally millions of men to the idea of a purely economic structure of society. One may easily conclude from an ex-

## Lecture II

tension of the ideas sketched here that the individual ownership of the means of production therefore means the end of man's future evolution, that there must be common ownership and common administration of the means of production by the workers.—Expropriation of the means of production has become the ideal of the working class.

It is most important not to become the prisoner of fixed ideas which are unrelated to reality, ideas which are still held by many members of the bourgeoisie who have been asleep to recent developments. For many of the dyed-in-the wool representatives of the bourgeoisie who are oblivious of the developments of recent decades still imagine that there are communists and social democrats who believe in sharing, in joint ownership, etcetera. They would be astonished to learn that millions of people have a carefully elaborated and clear-cut idea of how this is to be realized and must be realized, namely, by eliminating surplus value and bringing the means of production under common ownership. Every socialist agitator of today, every socialist 'stooge' laughs at the bourgeois who talks to them of communist and social-democratic aims, for he realizes that the central issue is the socialization of the means of production, the collective administration of the means of production. For, in the workers' eyes the source of slavery lies in the ownership of the means of production by isolated individuals, because he who is without the means of production is defenceless against the industrial employer who controls them.

The social struggle of modern times, therefore, is fundamentally the struggle for the ownership of the means of production. This struggle is inevitable since 'the history of all hitherto existing societies is the history of class struggles' (Marx in the Communist Manifesto). This is the third of the social-democratic tenets. The rise of the bourgeoisie was achieved at the expense of the feudal aristocracy. The rising

## From Symptom to Reality in Modern History

proletariat in its turn will take over the control and administration of the means of production and finally eliminate the bourgeoisie, just as the bourgeoisie had eliminated the aristocracy. History is the history of class struggles; the progress of mankind is determined by the victory of one class over another.

These three ideas—first, that material impulses alone determine the progress of mankind and the rest is simply ideological superstructure; secondly that the real evil is surplus value which can only be overcome by the collective ownership and administration of the means of production; and thirdly that the bourgeoisie must be overthrown, in the same way as the bourgeoisie had overthrown the old feudal aristocracy, in order that the means of production may become common property ... these are the three socialist doctrines which have gradually spread throughout the civilized world. And a significant symptom of recent years is this: the surviving members of the aristocracy and of the bourgeoisie have opted out, have picked up at most a few clichés such as 'sharing of goods', 'communism'—those clichés which are sometimes commented upon at length at the back of history books, though rarely is there a word about them in the text! People were oblivious of what had really happened; they were asleep whilst events took their course. And finally with great difficulty, under the compulsion of circumstances, under the influence of what has happened in the last four years (i.e. 1914–1918) a few people have begun to open their eyes. It is inconceivable how unaware people would have been but for the war, unaware that with every year thousands upon thousands were won over to the cause of socialism, never realizing that they were sitting on a volcano! It is disconcerting to have to admit that one is sitting on a volcano; people prefer to bury their heads in the

## Lecture II

sand. But that does not prevent the volcano from erupting and burying them alive.

I have here described a further symptom of contemporary history. This socialist conviction belongs to the symptoms of our time. It is a fact and not merely some vague theory. It is efficacious. I do not attach any importance to the solid body of the Lassallean[6] and Marxist theory, but I attach great importance to the fact that millions of men have chosen as their ideal to realize, as far as possible, what is advocated in the three tenets I have mentioned. This however is something which is radically opposed to the national element which, as I indicated earlier, was in some respect the founding father of modern history. Many things have developed out of this national element. Now the programme of the proletariat was first proclaimed in 1848 in the closing words of the Communist Manifesto, 'workers of the world unite'. There was scarcely a socialist meeting throughout the world that did not close with three cheers for international revolutionary socialism, republican social democracy. It was an international practice. And thus, alongside the internationalism of the Roman Church with its universalist idea there arose the Socialist International.[6] That is a fact, and these countless numbers of socialists are a fact. It is important to bear this in mind.

In order to conclude tomorrow—at least provisionally—this symptomatology of recent times we must pay close attention to the path which will enable us to follow the symptoms until they reveal to us to some extent the point where we can penetrate to the underlying reality. In addition to this we must recognize the fact that others have also created insoluble problems—you must feel how things develop, how they come to a head and end as insoluble problems! We saw how, in the nineteenth century, the trend towards a more liberal form of parliamentary government developed relatively peacefully in England; in France amidst political ferment and turmoil, or rather without motivation. And the further we move eastwards, the more we find that the national element is something imported, something transmitted from outside ... and this gives rise to insoluble problems. And that too is a symptom! The naïve imagine that there is a solution to everything. Now an insoluble problem of this nature (insoluble not to the abstract intellect, but insoluble in reality), was created 1870/71 between Western, Central and Eastern Europe—the problem of Alsace. The pundits of course know how to solve it— one state conquers the territory of its neighbour and the problem is solved. This has been tried by the one side or the other in the case of Alsace. Or if that solution is excluded, one can resort to the ballot box and the majority decides! That is simple enough. But those who are realists, who see more than one standpoint, who are aware that time is a real factor and that one cannot achieve in a short space of time what lies in the bosom of the future—in short, those who stand four square on the earth were aware that this was an insoluble problem. Read, for example, what was written, thought and said upon this problem in the seventies by those who attempted to throw light upon the future course of European evolution. They saw that what had happened in Alsace strangely anticipated later conditions in Europe, that the West would feel impelled to appeal to the East. At that time there were a few who were aware that the world would be confronted by the Slav problem because the West and Central Europe held different views upon the solution of this question. I only want to point out that this situation is an obvious symptom like that of the Thirty Years' War which I mentioned yesterday in order to show you that in history it is impossible to demonstrate that

## Lecture II

subsequent effects are the consequence of antecedent causes. The Thirty Years' War shows that the situation at the beginning, and before the outbreak of the war in 1618 was identical with the situation at the end of the war. The consequences of the war were unrelated to the antecedent causes; there can be no question therefore of cause and effect here (i.e. in the case of the Thirty Years' War). We have a characteristic symptom, and the same applies not only to the Alsatian problem, but also to many questions which have arisen in recent times. Problems are raised which do not lead to a solution, but to ever new conflicts and end in a blind alley. It is important to bear this in mind. These problems lead to such total deadlock that men cannot agree amongst themselves; opinions must differ because men inhabit different geographical regions in Europe. And it is a characteristic feature of the symptoms of recent history that men contrive to create situations that are incapable of solution.

We are now familiar with a whole series of features that are characteristic of the recent evolution of mankind—its sterility, the birth, in particular, of collective ideas which have no creative pretensions, such as the national impulse, for example. And in the midst of all this the continuous advance of the Consciousness Soul. We see everywhere problems that end in blind alleys, a characteristic feature of modern times. For what is discussed today, the measures undertaken by men today are to a large extent simply the revolving of the squirrel's cage. And a further characteristic is the attempt to damp down the consciousness, especially in relation to the Consciousness Soul which has to be developed. Nothing is more characteristic of our time than the lack of awareness amongst the educated section of the population of the real situation of the proletariat. They do not look beyond the external facade. Housewives complain that maidservants are unwilling to undertake certain duties; they seem unconcerned that not only factory workers, but also maidservants are saturated with Marxist theory. People are gradually beginning to talk of universal ideas of humanity in every shape and form. But if we show no concern for the individual and his welfare this is merely empty talk. For we must become aware of the important developments in evolution and we must take an active part in events.

I have felt compelled to draw your attention to this symptom of socialism, not in order to expound some particular social theory, but in order to present to you characteristic features of recent historical development.

We will continue our investigations tomorrow in order to round off this subject and to penetrate to the reality in isolated cases.

## LECTURE III

I have already indicated a few of the symptomatic forces that play a part in the development of contemporary history. I have only time to discuss a few of these impulses. To discuss them all—or even the most significant—would take us too far. I have been asked to give special attention to specific impulses of a symptomatic nature. This can be deferred until next week when I will willingly speak of those symptoms which have special reference to Switzerland and at the same time I will attempt to give a sketch of Swiss history.

Today, however, I propose to continue the studies we have already undertaken. I concluded my lecture yesterday with a picture, albeit a very inadequate picture, of the development in recent times of one of the most significant symptoms of contemporary history—socialism. Now for many who are earnestly seeking to discover the real motive forces of evolution, this social, or rather socialist movement occupies the focus of attention; apart from socialism they have never really considered the claims of anything else. Consequently people have failed in recent times to give adequate attention to the very important influence of something which tends to escape their notice. Even where they searched for new motives they paid no attention to those of a spiritual nature. If we ask how far people were aware of the impulses characteristic of modern evolution we can virtually discount from the outset those personalities who in the nineteenth century, and more especially in the twentieth century, were largely oblivious of contemporary evolution, who belonged to those circles which were indifferent to contemporary trends. The

*From Symptom to Reality in Modern History*

historians of the old upper classes were content to plough the old furrows, to record the genealogy of dynasties, the history of wars and perhaps other related material. It is true that studies in the history of civilization have been written, but these studies, from Buckle to Ratzel, take little account of the real driving forces of history. At the same time the proletariat was thirsting for knowledge and felt an ever-increasing desire for education. And this raised the three questions I mentioned yesterday. But the proletariat lacked the will to explore the more subtle interrelations of historical development. Consequently, up to the present, a historical symptom that has not been sufficiently emphasized is the historical significance of the natural scientific mode of thinking.

One can of course speak of the scientific mode of thinking in terms of its content or in relation to the transformation of modern thinking. But it is important to consider in what respect this scientific thinking has become a historical symptom like the others I have mentioned—the national impulse, the accumulation of insoluble political problems, etcetera. In fact, since the beginning of the epoch of the Consciousness Soul, the scientific mode of thinking has steadily increased amongst wide sections of the population. It is a mistake to imagine that only those think scientifically who have some acquaintance with natural science. That is quite false; in fact the reverse is true. Natural scientists think scientifically because that is the tendency of the vast majority of people today. People think in this way in the affairs of daily life— the peasant in the fields, the factory worker at his bench, the financier when he undertakes financial transactions. Everywhere we meet with scientific thinking and that is why scientists themselves have gradually adopted this mode of thought. It is necessary to rectify a popular misconception on this subject. It is not the mode of thinking of scientists or

## Lecture III

even of monistic visionaries that must engage our attention, but the mode of thinking of the general public. For natural science cannot provide a sufficiently powerful counterpoise to the universalist impulse of the church of Rome. What provides this counterpoise is a universal thinking that is in conformity with the laws of nature. And we must study this impulse as symptom in relation to the future evolution of modern man.

Text-books of history, rather thoughtlessly, usually date the birth of modern times from the discovery of America and the invention of gunpowder and printing, etcetera. If we take the trouble to study the course of recent history we realize that these symptomatic events—the discovery of America, the invention of gunpowder, and the art of printing, etcetera—did in fact inspire seamen and adventurers to pioneer voyages of exploration, that they popularized and diffused traditional knowledge, but that fundamentally they did not change the substance of European civilization in the ensuing centuries. We realize that the old political impulses which were revived in the different countries nonetheless remained the same as before because they were unable to derive any notable benefit from these voyages of discovery. In the newly discovered countries they simply resorted to conquest as they had formerly done in other territories: they mined and transported gold and so enriched themselves. In the sphere of printing they were able increasingly to control the apparatus of censorship. But the political forces of the past were unable to derive anything in the nature of a decisive impulse from these discoveries which were said to mark the birth of modern times. It was through the fusion of the scientific mode of thinking—after it had achieved certain results—with these earlier inventions and discoveries in which science had played no part that the really significant impulse of modern times arose. The colonizing activities of the various countries in modern times would be unthinkable without the contributions of modern science. The modern urge for colonization was the consequence of the achievements of natural science in the technical field. It was only possible to conquer foreign territories, as colonization was destined to do with the aid of scientific inventions, with the application of scientific techniques. These colonizing activities therefore first arose in the eighteenth century when natural science began to be transformed into technics.

Applied science marks the beginning of the machine age, and with it a new era of colonization which gradually spreads over the whole world. With technics an extremely important impulse of modern evolution is born in the Consciousness Soul. Those who understand the determinative factors here are aware that the impulses behind worldwide colonial expansion, that these colonizing activities and aspirations are directly related to the epoch of the Consciousness Soul. This epoch, as you know, will end in the third millenium, to be followed by the epoch of the Spirit Self, and will as the result of colonization bring about a different configuration of mankind throughout the world. Now the epoch of the Consciousness Soul recognizes that there are so-called civilized and highly civilized men, and others who are extremely primitive—so primitive that Rousseau was captivated by their primitive condition and elaborated his theory of the 'noble savage'. In the course of the epoch of the Consciousness Soul this differentiation will cease—*how* it will cease we cannot now discuss in detail. But it is the function of the Consciousness Soul to end this differentiation which is a heritage from the past.

Armed with this knowledge we see the connection between wars such as the American Civil War and modern colonizing activities in their true light. When we bear in mind the importance of these colonizing activities for the epoch of

## Lecture III

the Consciousness Soul then we gain insight into the full significance of isolated symptoms in this field. And these colonizing activities are inconceivable without the support of scientific thinking.

We must really give heed to this scientific thinking, if, from the point of view of the fifth post-Atlantean epoch, the epoch of the Consciousness Soul, we wish to penetrate to the true reality of human evolution. It is a characteristic of this modern scientific thinking that it can only apprehend the 'corpse' of reality, the phantom. We must be quite clear about this, for it is important. The scientific method starts from observation and proceeds to experimentation, and this applies in all spheres. Now there is a vast difference between the observation of nature and the knowledge which is confirmed by experimental proof. Observation of nature—with different nuances—was common to all epochs. But when man observes nature he becomes one with nature and shares in the life of nature. But, strangely enough, this communion with nature blunts the consciousness to some extent. One cannot live the life of nature and at the same time know or cognize in the sense in which the modern Consciousness Soul understands this term. One cannot do both at the same time any more than one can be asleep and awake at the same time. If one wishes to live in communion with nature one must be prepared in a certain sense to surrender one's consciousness to nature. And that is why the observation of nature cannot fathom its secrets, because when man observes nature his consciousness is somewhat dimmed and the secrets of nature escape him. In order to apprehend the secrets of nature he must be alive to the supersensible.

One cannot develop the Consciousness Soul in a semi-conscious state, a state of diminished consciousness, and therefore modern natural science quite instinctively attempts to dispense with observation and to depend upon experimentation for its findings. Experiments have been undertaken even in the fields of biology and anthropology. Now in experimentation the first consideration is to select and assemble the material, to determine the order of procedure. In experimental embryology for example, the order of procedure is determined not by nature but by intellection or human intelligence; it is determined by an intellectual faculty which is detached from nature and is centred in man. 'We murder to dissect'—our knowledge of nature is derived from experimental investigation. Only what is acquired experimentally can be exploited technically. Knowledge of nature only becomes ripe for technical exploitation when it has passed through the indirect process of experimentation. The knowledge of nature which hitherto had been introduced into social life had not yet reached the stage of technics. It would be monstrous to speak of technics unless it is concerned purely with the application of experimentation to the social order or to what serves the social order.

Thus modern man introduces into the social order the results of experimental knowledge in the form of technics; that is to say, he brings in the forces of death. Let us not forget that we bring forces of death into our colonizing activities; that when we construct machines for industry, or submit the worker to the discipline of the machine we are introducing forces of death. And death permeates our modern historical structure when we extend our monetary economy to larger or smaller territories and when we seek to build a social order on the pattern of modern science as we have instinctively done today. And whenever we introduce natural science into our community life we introduce at all times the forces of death that are self destructive.

This is one of the most important symptoms of our time. We can make honest and sincere pronouncements—I do

## Lecture III

not mean merely rhetorical pronouncements—about the great scientific achievements of modern times and the benefits they have brought to technics and to our social life. But these are only half truths, for fundamentally all these achievements introduce into contemporary life an unmistakably moribund element which is incapable of developing of itself. The greatest acquisitions of civilization since the fifteenth century are doomed to perish if left to themselves. And this is inescapable. The question then arises: if modern technics is simply a source of death, as it must inevitably be, why did it arise? Certainly not in order to provide mankind with the spectacle of machines and industry, but for a totally different reason. It arose precisely because of the seeds of death it bore within it; for if man is surrounded by a moribund, mechanical civilization it is only by reacting against it that he can develop the Consciousness Soul. So long as man lived in communion with nature, i.e. before the advent of the machine age, he was open to suggestion because he was not fully conscious. He was unable to be fully self-sufficient because he had not yet experienced the forces of death. Ego-consciousness and the forces of death are closely related. I have already tried to show this in a variety of ways: In ideation and cognition, for example, man is no longer in contact with the life-giving, vitalizing forces within him; he is given over to the forces of organic degeneration. I have tried to show that we owe the possibility of conscious thought to the process of organic degeneration, to the processes of destruction and death. If we could not develop in ourselves 'cerebral hunger', that is to say, processes of catabolism, of degeneration and disintegration, we could not behave as intelligent beings, we should be vacillating, indecisive creatures living in a semiconscious, dream-like state. We owe our intellect to the degenerative processes of the brain. And the epoch of the

*From Symptom to Reality in Modern History*

Consciousness Soul must provide man with the opportunity to experience disintegration in his environment. We do not owe the development of modern, conscious thinking to a superabundant vitality. This conscious thinking, this very core of man's being grew and developed because it was imbued with the forces of death inherent in modern technology, in modern industry and finance. And that is what the life of the Consciousness Soul demanded.

And this phenomenon is seen in other spheres. Let us recur to the impulses to which I drew attention earlier. Let us consider the case of England where we saw how a specific form of parliamentary government develops as a certain tendency through the centuries, how the self-dependent personality seeks to realize itself. The personality wishes to emancipate itself and to become self-sufficient. It wishes to play a part in the life of the community and at the same time to affirm its independence. The parliamentary system of government is only one means of affirming the personality. But when the individual who participates in parliamentary government asserts himself, the moment he sacrifices his will to the vote he surrenders his personality. And, rightly understood, the rise of parliamentary government in England in the centuries following upon the civil wars of the fifteenth century provides ample evidence of this. In the early years of the democratic system society was based upon a class structure, the various classes or 'estates' not only wishing to affirm their class status, but to express their views through the ballot-box. They were free to speak; but people are not satisfied with speeches and mutual agreement, they want to vote. When one votes, when speeches are followed by voting, one kills what lives in the soul even whilst one speaks. Thus every form of parliamentary government ends in levelling down, in egalitarianism. It is born of the affirmation of the personality and ends with the suppression of the personality.

## Lecture III

This situation is inescapable; affirmation of the personality leads to suppression of the personality. It is a cyclic process like life itself which begins with birth and ends in death. In the life of man birth and death are two distinct moments in time; in the life of history, the one is directly related to the other, birth and death are commixed and commingled. We must never lose sight of this.

I do not wish you to take these remarks as a criticism of parliamentary government. That would be tantamount to insinuating that I said: since man is born only to die he ought never to have been born—which is absurd. One should not impute to the world such foolishness—that it permits man to be born only to die. Please do not accuse me of saying that parliamentary government is absurd because the personality which gives birth to this system proceeds to destroy the system which it has itself created. I simply wish to relate it directly to life, to that which is common to all life—birth and death, thus showing that it is something that is closely associated with reality. At the same time I want to show you the characteristic feature of all external phenomena of a like nature in the epoch of the Consciousness Soul, for they are all subject to birth and death.

Now in the inner circles of the occult lodges of the English speaking world it has often been said: let us not reveal to the world the mystery of birth and death, for in so doing we shall betray to the uninitiated the nature of the modern epoch! We shall transmit to them a knowledge that we wish to reserve for ourselves. Therefore it was established as the first rule of the masonic lodges never to speak openly of the mystery of birth and death, to conceal the fact that this mystery is omnipresent, above all in historical phenomena. For to speak of this is to open the eyes of the public to the tragedy of modern life which will gradually be compelled— a compulsion to which it will not easily submit—to divert man's attention from the results of work to the work itself. One must find joy in work, saying to oneself: the external rewards of work in the present epoch serve the purposes of death and not of creative life. If one is unwilling to further the forces of death, one cannot work with modern techniques, for today man is the servant of the machine. He who rejects the machine simply wishes to return to the past.

Study the history of France and the attempts made to thrust inwards the emancipation of the personality, ending in that disastrous suppression of the personality which we observe in the final phase of the French Revolution and in the rise of Napoleonism. Or take the case of Italy. From what hidden springs did modern Italy derive that dynamic energy which inflamed the nationalism to the point of *sacro egoismo*? One must probe beneath the surface in order to discover the factors underlying world events. Recall for a moment that important moment before the birth of the Consciousness Soul. This dynamic energy peculiar to modern Italy is derived in all its aspects from that which the Papacy had implanted in the Italian soul. The significance of the Papacy for Italy lies in the fact that it has gradually imbued the Italian soul with its own spirit. And, as so often happens to the magician's apprentice, the result was not what was intended—a violent reaction against the Papacy itself in modern Italy. Here we see how that for which one strives provokes its own destruction. Not the thoughts, but the forces of sensibility and enthusiasm, even those which inspired Garibaldi, are relics of the one-time Catholic fervour —but when these forces changed direction they turned against Catholicism.

People will understand the present epoch only if they grasp the right relationship between these things. Europe witnessed those various symptomatic events which I have described to you. And in the East, as if in the background,

## Lecture III

we see the configuration of Russia, welded out of the remnants of the Byzantine ecclesiastical framework, out of the Nordic-Slavonic racial impulse and out of Asianism which is diffused in a wide variety of forms over Eastern Europe. But this triad is uncreative; it does not emanate from the Russian soul itself, nor is it characteristic of that which lives in the Russian soul. What is it that offers the greatest imaginable contrast to the emancipation of the personality?—The Byzantine element. A great personality of modern times who is much underrated is Pobjedonoszeff. He was an eminent figure who was steeped in the Byzantine tradition. He could only desire the reverse of what the epoch of the Consciousness Soul seeks to achieve and of what it develops naturally in man. Even if the Byzantine element had made deeper inroads into Russian orthodoxy, even if this element which stifles everything personal and individual had gained an even stronger hold ... the sole consequence nonetheless would have been a powerful age for the emancipation of the personality. If, in the study of modern Russian history, you do not read of those events which it has always been forbidden to record, then you will not have a true picture of Russian history, you will be unaware of the really living element. If however you read the official version, the only version permitted hitherto by the authorities, you will find everything which pervades Russian life as an instrument of death. It appears here in its most characteristic form because Russian life is richest in future promise. And because Russian life bears within it the seeds of the development of the Spirit Self, all the external achievements of the era of the Consciousness Soul hitherto bring only death and destruction. And this had to be, since what seeks to develop as Spirit Self needs the substratum of death.

We must recognize that this is a necessity for the evolution

*From Symptom to Reality in Modern History*

of the Consciousness Soul, otherwise we shall never grasp the real needs of our time. We shall be unable to form a clear picture of the destructive forces which have overtaken mankind if we are unaware that the events of these last four years are simply an epitome of the forces of death that have pervaded the life of mankind since the birth of the epoch of the Consciousness Soul.

Characteristically the dead hand of scientific thinking has exercised a strange influence upon one of the most prophetic personalities of recent time. In contemporary history the following incident is symptomatic and will always remain memorable. In the year 1830 in Weimar, Soret[1] visited Goethe who received him with some excitement—I mean he betrayed excitement in his demeanour—but not with deep emotion. Goethe said to Soret: 'At last the controversy has come to a head, everything is in flames'. He made a few additional remarks which led Soret to believe that Goethe was referring to the revolution which had broken out in Paris in 1830 and he answered him accordingly. But Goethe replied: 'I am not referring to the revolution; that is not particularly important. What is important is the controversy between Cuvier and Geoffroy de Saint-Hilaire in the Academy of Sciences of Paris'—Cuvier was a representative of the old school which simply compares and classifies organisms—a way of looking at nature that is concerned above all with technique—whilst Geoffroy de Saint-Hilaire has a living conception of the whole course of evolution. Goethe saw Saint-Hilaire as the leader of a new school of scientific thinking, different from that of Copernicus, Kepler and Galileo. Cuvier belongs to the old school of thought; Geoffroy de Saint-Hilaire is the representative of a scientific outlook which sees nature as a living organism. Therefore Goethe saw the dawn of a new epoch when Geoffroy de Saint-Hilaire prepared the ground for a new scientific think-

## Lecture III

ing which, when fully developed, must lead to a supersensible interpretation of nature and ultimately to supersensible, clairvoyant knowledge. For Goethe this was the revolution of 1830, not the political events in Paris. Thus Goethe showed himself to be one of the most prescient spirits of his time. He showed that he sensed and felt what was the cardinal issue of our time.

Today we must have the courage to look facts squarely in the face, a courage of which earlier epochs had no need. We must have the courage to follow closely the course of events, for it is important that the Consciousness Soul can fulfil its development. In earlier epochs the development of the Consciousness Soul was not important. Because the Consciousness Soul is of paramount importance in the present epoch, everything that man creates in the social sphere must be consciously planned. Consequently his social life can no longer be determined by the old instinctive life; nor can he introduce solely the achievements of natural science into social life for these are forces of death and are unable to quicken life; they are simply dead-sea fruit and sow destruction such as we have seen in the last four years. In the present epoch the following is important.

Sleep, of course, is a necessity for man. In waking life he is in control of his normal free will . . . he can make use of this free will for the various things he encounters through Lucifer and Ahriman, in order to develop guide-lines for the future. When he falls asleep this so called free will ceases to function; he continues to think without knowing it, but his thinking is no less efficacious. Thinking does not cease on falling asleep, it continues until the moment of waking. One simply forgets this in the moment of waking up. We are therefore unaware of the power of those thoughts that pour into the human soul from the moment of falling asleep until the moment of waking up. But let us remember that for the epoch of the Consciousness Soul the gods have abandoned the human soul during sleep. In earlier epochs the gods instilled into the human soul between sleeping and waking what they chose to impart. If they had continued to act in this way man would not have become a free being. Consequently he is now open to all kinds of other influences between sleeping and waking. At a pinch we can live our waking life with natural science and its achievements, but they are of no avail in sleep and death. We can only think scientifically during our waking hours. The moment we fall asleep, scientific thinking is meaningless—as meaningless as speaking French in a country where no one understands a word of French. In sleep only that language has significance which one acquires through supersensible knowledge, the language which has its source in the supersensible. Supersensible knowledge must take the place of what the gods in former times had implanted in the instinctive life. The purpose of the present epoch of the Consciousness Soul is this: man must open himself to supersensible impulses and penetrate to a knowledge of reality. To believe that everything that our present age has produced and still produces without the support of supersensible impulses is something living and creative and not impregnated with the forces of death is to harbour an illusion, just as it is an illusion to believe that a woman can bear a child without fecundation. Without impregnation a woman today remains sterile and dies without issue. Modern civilization in the form it has developed since the beginning of the fifteenth century and especially in respect of its outstanding achievements, is destined to remain sterile unless fertilized henceforth by impulses from the supersensible world. Everything that is not fertilized by spiritual impulses is doomed to perish. In this epoch of the Consciousness Soul, though you may introduce democracy, parliamentary government, modern

## Lecture III

finance economy, modern industrialism, though you may introduce the principle of nationality the world over, though you may advocate all those principles on which men base what they call the new order—a subject on which they descant like drunken men who have no idea what they are talking about—all these things will serve only the forces of death unless they are fructified by spiritual impulses. All that we must inevitably create today, forces that bring death in all domains, will only be of value if we learn how to transform these forces by our insights into the supersensible.

Let us realize the seriousness of this situation and let us remember—as we have learnt from our study of the symptoms of recent history—that what man considers to be his greatest achievements, natural science, sociology, modern industrial techniques and modern finance economy, all date from the fifteenth century. These are destructive agents unless fructified by spiritual impulses. Only then can they advance the evolution of mankind. Then they have positive value; in themselves they are detrimental. Of all that mankind today extols, not without a certain pride and presumption, as his greatest achievements, nothing is good in itself; it is only of value when permeated with spirit.

This is not an arbitrary expression of opinion, but a lesson we learn from a study of the symptoms of modern history. The time has now come when we must develop individual consciousness. And we must also be aware of what we may demand of this consciousness. The moment we begin to dogmatize, even unwittingly, we impede the development of the consciousness. I must therefore remind you once again of the following incident. I happened to be giving a course of lectures in Hamburg on *The Bible and Wisdom*.* Amongst the audience were two Catholic priests. Since I had said nothing of a polemical nature which could

* 5th December, 1908. See Bibl. Nr. 68.

## From Symptom to Reality in Modern History

offend a Catholic priest and since they were not the type of Jesuit who is a watchdog of the Church and whose function is to stick his fingers in every pie, but ordinary parish priests, they approached me after the lecture and said: we too preach purgatory; you also speak of a time of expiation after death. We preach paradise; you speak of the conscious experience of the Spirit; fundamentally there are no objections to the content of your teaching. But they would certainly have found ample grounds for objection if they had gone more deeply into the matter—a single lecture of course did not suffice for this. And they continued: You see the difference between us is this: You address yourself to a certain section of the population which is already familiar with the premises of anthroposophy, people who are educated and are conversant with certain concepts and ideas. We, on the other hand speak to all men, we speak a language which everyone can understand. And that is the right approach—to speak for all men. Whereupon I replied: Reverend fathers (I always believe in respecting titles) what you are saying is beside the point. I do not doubt that you believe you speak for all men, that you can choose your words in such a way as to give the impression that you are speaking for all men. But that is a subjective judgement, is it not? that is what one usually says in self-justification. What is important is not whether we believe we speak for all men, but the facts, the objective reality. And now I should like to ask you, in an abstract theoretical way: what evidence is there that I do not speak for all men? You claim to speak for all men and no doubt there are arguments that would support your claim. But I ask you for the facts. Do all those for whom you think you are able to speak still attend your church today? That is the real question. Of course my two interlocutors could not claim that everyone attended their church regularly. You see, I continued, that I am concerned with the facts. I speak

## Lecture III

for those who are outside the church, who also have the right to be led to the Christ. I realize that amongst them there are those who want to hear of the Christ impulse one way or another. That is a reality. And what matters is the reality, not personal opinions.

It is most desirable to base one's opinions on facts and not on subjective impressions; for, in the epoch of the Consciousness Soul nothing is more dangerous than to surrender to, or show a predilection for personal opinions or prejudices. In order to develop the Consciousness Soul we must not allow ourselves to become dogmatists unwittingly; the driving forces of our thoughts and actions must be determined by facts. That is important. Beneath the surface of historical evolution there is a fundamental conflict between the acceptance of what we consider to be right and the compulsion of facts. And this is of particular importance when studying history, for we shall never have a true picture of history unless we see history as a truly great teacher. We must not force the facts to fit history, but allow history to speak for itself. In this respect the whole world has forgotten much in the last four years. Facts are scarcely allowed to speak for themselves; we only hear what we deem to be facts. And this situation will persist for a long time. And it will be equally long before we develop the capacity to apprehend reality objectively. In the epoch of the Consciousness Soul what matters in all spheres of life is an objective apprehension of reality; we must strive to acquire an impartial attitude to reality.

What our epoch demands—if we wish gradually to look beyond the symptoms of history (I will speak more of this in my next lectures)—is that we turn our attention to those spiritual forces which can restore man's creativity. For, as we have seen, the most characteristic feature of all phenomena today is a decline in creativity. Man must open himself

## From Symptom to Reality in Modern History

to the influences of the supersensible world so that what his Spirit Self prepares may enter into his ego; otherwise the paths to the Spirit Self would be closed to him. Man therefore must familiarize himself with that which is pure spirit, with that which can penetrate to the centre of his psychic life. The moment he is prepared to turn his attention to this centre of his soul life through a sensible study of the symptoms in history, he will also be prepared to examine more objectively the events at the periphery.

In man there exists a polarity—the psychic centre and the periphery. As he penetrates ever more deeply into his psychic and spiritual life he reaches this centre. In this centre he must open himself to those historical impulses which I have already described to you. Here he will feel an ever increasing urge for the spirit if he wishes to become acquainted with historical reality. In return however, he will also feel a desire to strive towards the opposite pole at the periphery. He will develop an understanding for what is pressing towards the periphery—his somatic nature. If in order to understand history we must look inward, as I have indicated, to the underlying symptoms, then in order to understand medicine, for example, hygiene and medical health services we must look outwards, to cosmic rhythms for the source of pathological symptoms.

Just as modern history fails to penetrate to spiritual realities, so modern medicine, modern hygiene and medical health services fail to penetrate to the symptoms which are of cosmic provenance. I have often emphasized the fact that the individual cannot help his neighbour, however deep his insight into current problems, because today they are in the hands of those who are looking for the wrong solution. They must become the responsibility of those who are moving in the right direction. Clearly, just as the external facts are true that the outward aspect of James I was such and such,

## Lecture III

as I pointed out earlier, so, from the external point of view it is also true that a certain kind of bacillus is connected with the present influenza epidemic. But if it is true, for example, that rats are carriers of the bubonic plague, one cannot say that rats are responsible for the plague. People have always imagined that the bubonic plague was spread by rats. But bacilli, as such, are of course in no way connected with disease. In phenomena of this kind we must realize that just as behind the symptoms of history we are dealing with psychic and spiritual experiences, so too behind somatic symptoms we are dealing with experiences of a cosmological order. In other cases the situation of course will be different! What is especially important here is the rhythmic course of cosmic events, and it is this that we must study. We must ask ourselves: In what constellation were we living when, in the nineties, the present influenza epidemic appeared in its benign form? In what cosmic constellation are we living at the present time? By virtue of what cosmic rhythm does the influenza epidemic of the nineties appear in a more acute form today? Just as we must look for a rhythm behind a series of historical symptoms, so we must look for a rhythm behind the appearance of certain epidemics.

In the solfatara regions of Italy one need only hold a naked flame over the fango hole and immediately gases and steam escape from the dormant volcano. This shows that if one performs a certain action above the surface of the earth nature reacts by producing these effects. Do you regard it as impossible that something takes place in the sun—since its rays are directed daily towards the earth—which has significance for the earth emanations and is related to the life of man, and that this reaction varies according to the different geographical localities? Do you think that we shall have any understanding of these matters unless we are prepared to

## From Symptom to Reality in Modern History

accept a true cosmology founded upon a knowledge of the soul and spirit? The statement that man's inclination to resort to war is connected with the periodic appearance of sun spots is, of course, regarded as absurd. But there comes a point when statements of this kind cease to be absurd, when certain pathological manifestations in the emotional life are seen to be connected with cosmological phenomena such as the periodic appearance of sun spots. And when tiny creatures, these petty tyrants—bacilli or rats—really transmit from one human being to another something that is related to the cosmos, then this transmission is only a secondary phenomenon. This can be easily demonstrated and consequently finds wide public support—but it is not the main issue. And we shall not come to terms with the main issue unless we have the will to study the peripheral symptoms as well.

I do not believe that men will acquire a more reasonable and catholic view of history unless they study historical symptomatology in the light of supersensible knowledge which is so necessary for mankind today. Men will only achieve results in the sphere of health, hygiene and medicine if they study not historical, but cosmological symptoms. For the diseases we suffer on earth are visitations from heaven. In order to understand this we must abandon the preconceived ideas which are prevalent today. We have an easy explanation: a God is omnipresent . . . but whilst recognizing the presence of God in history mankind today is unable to explain the manifold retardative or harmful phenomena in history. And when we are faced with a situation like the last four years (1914–1918), then this business of the single God in history becomes extremely dubious, for this God of history has the curious habit of multiplying, and each nation defends its national God and provokes other nations by claiming the superiority of its own God. And when

## Lecture III

we are expected to look to cosmology and at the same time remain comfortably attached to this single God, then this same God inflicts disease upon us. But when we can rise to the idea of the trinity, God, Lucifer and Ahriman, when we are aware of this trinity in the supersensible world behind the historical symptoms, when we know that this trinity is present in the cosmic universe, then there is no need to appeal to the 'good God'. We then know that heaven visits disease upon us by virtue of its association with the earth, just as I can evoke sulphur fumes by holding a naked flame over a solfatara. We can only advance the cause of progress in the epoch of the Consciousness Soul, when men recognize the validity of spiritual realities. Therefore everything depends upon this one aim: the search, the quest for truth.

## LECTURE IV

Before turning to other matters I must speak of certain wider conceptions that follow from our consideration of the recent development of human history. We attempted to examine this development from the stand-point of a symptomatology; we tried to show that what are usually called historical facts are not the essential elements in history, but that they are symbols of the true reality that lies behind them. This true reality, at least in the sphere of the historical evolution of mankind, is thus detached from what can be perceived in the phenomenal world, i.e. the so-called historical facts. If we do not regard the so-called historical facts as the true reality but seek in them manifestations of something that lies behind them then we discover of course a supersensible element.

In studying history it is not easy to show the true nature of the supersensible because people believe, when they discover certain thoughts or ideas in history, or when they record historical events, that they are already in touch with the supersensible. We must be quite clear that whatever the phenomenal world presents to the senses, to the intellect or emotions cannot in any way be regarded as supersensible. Therefore everything that is normally depicted as history belongs to the sensible world. Of course when we study the symptomatology of history we shall not regard the symptoms as having equal value; the study itself will show that, in order to arrive at the supersensible reality behind the events, a particular symptom is of capital importance, whilst other symptoms are perhaps of no importance.

## Lecture IV

I have already mentioned many of the more or less important symptoms manifested since mankind entered the epoch of the Consciousness Soul. I should now like to try to describe to you, step by step, a few characteristics of the supersensible present in the background. Some I have already described. For of course a fundamental feature pulsing in the supersensible is the entrance of mankind into the civilization of the Consciousness Soul, that is to say, the acquisition of the organs necessary for the development of the Consciousness Soul. That is the essential. But we have recently seen that the other pole, the complement to this inner elaboration of the Consciousness Soul, must be the aspiration to a revelation from the spiritual world. Men must realize that henceforth they will be unable to progress spiritually unless they open themselves to the new revelation of the supersensible world.

Let us now consider these two poles of evolution. To a certain extent they have come to the fore in the centuries since 1413 when mankind entered the epoch of the Consciousness Soul. These two impulses will continue to develop, will assume a wide diversity of forms in the different epochs up to the third millennium and will be responsible for the manifold vicissitudes that befall mankind. Individuals will gradually become aware of this. In considering these two impulses in particular, we learn that fundamental changes have occurred since the fifteenth century. Today we are in a position to draw attention to these important developments. In the eighteenth century, and even in the early nineteenth century it would not have been possible to show the operation of these two impulses purely from the observation of external phenomena. They had not yet been operative for a sufficient length of time to show their full effect. Now such is their dynamic power that it is perceptible in external phenomena.

Let us now consider an essential fact which has an

important bearing today. Whilst early indications were apparent only to those who were more or less acquainted with the true state of affairs—I am referring to the Russian Revolution in its last phase, namely from October 1917 to the peace negotiations of Brest-Litovsk—this extraordinarily interesting development which can easily be followed, since it lasted only a few months, is of immense importance to those who seriously wish to understand the historical symptoms, for this development is of course a historical symptom. In the final analysis the origin of the Russian Revolution is to be found in the deeper impulses of contemporary evolution. In this revolution it is a question of new ideas. For when we speak of real evolution in mankind we are concerned only with new ideas. Everything else—as we have already indicated, and we will recur to this later—is subject to a certain extent to the symptoms of death. It is a question of making new ideas effective. As you will have gathered from the many discussions which I have had upon this subject over recent decades—these new ideas must be able to capture the broad masses of peasantry in Eastern Europe. Of course we are dealing here with a passivity of soul, but a soul that, as you know, is receptive especially to new and modern ideas, for the simple reason that it bears within it the seed of the Spirit Self. Whereas, on the whole, the rest of the world's population bears within it the impulse to develop the Consciousness Soul, the broad mass of the Russian population, together with a few satellites, bears within it the seed from which the Spirit Self will be developed in the course of the sixth post-Atlantean epoch. This necessitates, of course, very special circumstances. But this has an important bearing on what we are about to study next.

   Now this idea—partly correct, partly false or wholly mistaken—this modern idea of something entirely new which was destined to capture the broad mass of the population

## Lecture IV

could only come from those who had had the opportunity to be educated, namely from the ruling classes.

After the fall of Czarism the centre of the stage was at first occupied by an element that was closely connected with a totally sterile class, the upper middle class—called in the West, heavy industry, etcetera. This could only be an interlude which we need not discuss, for this class is destitute of ideas and, as a class, is of course quite incapable of developing ideas. (When speaking of these matters I never indulge in personalities.)

Now at first those elements which were of middle class origin, together with a sprinkling of working class elements, formed the party of the left. They formed the leading wing of the so-called Social Revolutionaries and were gradually joined by the Mensheviks. They were men who—purely in terms of their numbers—could easily have played a leading part in determining the future course of the Russian Revolution. As you know events took a different course. The radical wing of the Russian Social Democratic party, the Bolsheviks, took over the helm. When they (the Bolsheviks) came to power, the Social Revolutionaries, the Mensheviks and their followers in the West were quite sure that the whole charade would not last more than a week before everything collapsed. Well, the Bolsheviks have now been in power more than a week and you can rest assured of this: if many prophets are bad prophets, then those who today base their predictions of historical events upon the outmoded world conceptions of certain middle classes are certainly the worst! What is the cause of this situation? This problem of the October Revolution, throughout the months following its outbreak and until today, is, in the terminology of physics, not a problem of pressure, but of suction. It is important that we can infer from the historical situation that we are dealing here not with a problem of pressure, but of suction. What do we understand by a problem of suction? As you know, when we create a vacuum by sucking out the air in the glass jar of an airpump and then remove the stopper, the air rushes in with a hissing sound. The air rushes in, not of its own volition, but because a vacuum has been created.

This was the situation of those elements which to some extent stood midway between the peasantry and the Bolsheviks, between the Social Revolutionaries, the Mensheviks, and the radical revolutionary groups of the extreme left, i.e. the Petrograd Soviet. What had happened was that the Mensheviks, though they had an overwhelming majority in the Provisional Government were totally destitue of ideas. They had not a word to say about the future of mankind. No doubt they cherished touching ethical sentiments and other romantic ideals, but, as I have often pointed out, ethical good intentions do not provide the impulses which can further the development of mankind. Thus a vacuum was created, an ideological vacuum, and the radical left wing rushed in. It is impossible to believe that, by their very nature, the most radical socialist elements who were alien to Russian tradition and culture were destined to take over in Russia. They could never have done so if the Social Revolutionaries and the various groups associated with them had had any ideas of how to give a lead. But you will ask: what ideas ought they to have had? A fruitful answer can only be found today by those who are no longer afraid to face this fact: for this section of the population the only fertile ideas are those which spring from spiritual experience. Nothing else avails.

It is true that these people have become more or less radical and will now deny their middle class origin, many at least will deny it, but there is no mistaking their origin. But the essential point is that this section of the population which created a vacuum, who were bereft of ideas, simply could

## Lecture IV

not be induced to develop anything in the nature of positive ideas.

And this applies, of course, not only to Russia. But the Russian Revolution in its final phase—provisionally the final phase—demonstrates this fact with particular clarity to those who are prepared to study the matter. We see how, day after day, these people (i.e. the Mensheviks and their supporters) who have created a vacuum are gradually forced back and how others rush in to fill the vacuum, i.e. to replace them. But today this phenomenon is world-wide. The fact is that the section of the population which today stands politically between the right and the left has steadily refused to make the slightest effort to develop a positive *Weltanschauung*. In our epoch of the Consciousness Soul a creative *Weltanschauung* must of necessity be one which also promotes social cohesion.

It was this which from the very beginning permeated our Anthroposophical movement. It was not intended in any way to be a sectarian movement, but endeavoured to come to terms with the impulse of our time, with everything that is essential and important for mankind today. This was increasingly our goal. It is this which is most difficult to bring to men's understanding today for the simple reason that the belief persists (not in all, but in the majority) that what they are looking for in Anthroposophy, as they understand it, is a little moral uplift, something necessary for one's private and personal edification, something which insulates one from the serious matters which are settled in Parliament, in the Federal Councils, in this or that Corporation, or even round the beer table. What we must realize is that the whole of life must be impregnated with ideas which can be derived only from spiritual science.

Whilst this section of the population, i.e. the bourgeoisie, was indifferent to spiritual ideas, the proletariat showed and

97

## From Symptom to Reality in Modern History

still shows today a lively interest in them. But as a consequence of the historical evolution of modern times the horizon of the proletariat is limited purely to the sensible world. It is prisoner of materialistic impulses and seeks to steer the evolution of mankind into utilitarian channels. The bourgeoisie knows only empty rhetoric, what it is pleased to call its *Weltanschauung* is simply verbiage, because it has no roots in contemporary life and is a survival from earlier times. The proletariat, on the other hand, because it is motivated by a totally new economic impulse lives therefore in realities, but only in realities of a sensible nature.

This provides us with an important criterion. In the course of the last few centuries the life of mankind has undergone a fundamental change; we have entered the machine age. The life of the middle class and the upper middle class has scarcely felt the impact of the machine age. For the new and powerful influences which have affected the life of the bourgeoisie in recent centuries belong to the pre-machine age ... for example, the introduction of coffee as the favourite beverage for café gossip. Equally the new banking practices, etcetera, introduced by the bourgeoisie are wholly unsuited to the new impulses of today. They are simply a hotchpotch of the ancient usages formerly practised in commercial life.

On the other hand the proletariat of today is the caste or class which is dominated by a modern impulse in the external life and to a certain extent is the creation of modern impulses themselves. Since the invention of the spinning jenny and the mechanical loom in the eighteenth century, the entire political economy of mankind has been transformed, and these inventions have been largely responsible for the birth of the modern proletariat. The proletariat is a creation of the modern epoch, that is the point to bear in mind. The bourgeois is not a creation of modern times. For the class or

## Lecture IV

group which existed in earlier times and which could be compared with the proletariat of today did not belong to the third estate; it still formed part of the old patriarchal order. And the patriarchal order is totally different from the social order of the machine age. In this new order the proletarian is surrounded by a completely mechanized environment wholly divorced from living nature. He is entirely engaged in practical activities, but he thirsts for a *Weltanschauung* and he has endeavoured to model his conception of the universe on the pattern of a vast machine. For men see the universe as a reflection of their own environment. Now I have already pointed out there is an affinity between the theologian and the soldier. They see the universe as a battleground, the scene of the clash between the forces of good and evil, etcetera and leave it at that. Equally there is a close affinity between the jurist and the civil servant; they and the metaphysician see in the universe the realization of abstract ideas. Small wonder then that the proletarian sees the universe as a vast machine in which he is simply a cog. That is why he wishes to model the social order on the pattern of a vast machine.

But there was and still is a vast difference between, for example, the modern proletarian and the modern bourgeois—we can ignore the class which is already in decline. The modern bourgeois has not the slightest interest in deeper ideological questions, whereas the proletarian is passionately interested in them. It is true the modern bourgeois holds frequent meetings for an exchange of views, but for the most part they are so much hot air; the proletarian on the other hand discusses his daily life and working conditions and the daily output of mass production. When one passes from a middle class reunion to a proletarian meeting one has the following impression—In the former they spend time in discussing what a fine thing it would be if men lived in peace, if all were pacifists for example, or other fine sentiments of a

*From Symptom to Reality in Modern History*

like nature. But all this is merely verbal dialectic seasoned with a pinch of sentimentality. The bourgeoisie is not imbued with a desire to open a window on the universe, to realize their objectives from out of the mysteries of the Cosmos. When you attend a proletarian meeting you are immediately aware that the workers are talking of realities, even if they are the realities of the physical plane. They have the history of the working class at their finger-tips, from the invention of the mechanical loom and the spinning jenny until the present day. Every man has had dinned into him the history of those early beginnings and their subsequent development, and how the proletariat has become what it is today. How this situation arose is familiar ground to every worker who is actively involved in this development and who is not completely stupid, and there are few amongst this section of the population who haven't a good head on their shoulders.

One could give many typical instances of the obtuseness of the present bourgeoisie with regard to ideological questions. One need only recall how these people react when a poet presents on the stage figures from the supersensible world (those who are not poets dare not take this risk for fear of being labelled visionaries). The spectators half accept these figures because there is no need to believe in them, because they are totally unreal—they are merely poetic inventions! This situation has arisen in the course of the development of the epoch of the Consciousness Soul. If we consider this situation spatially, we see the growth of a section of the population which, unless it takes heed, is increasingly in danger of ending completely in empty talk. But one can also consider this same situation in relation to time, and in this respect I have repeatedly called attention from widely different angles to certain important moments in time.

The epoch of the Consciousness Soul began approximately

## Lecture IV

in 1413. In the forties of the nineteenth century, about 1840 or 1845, the first fifth of this era had already run its course. The forties were an important period. For the powers impelling world evolution foresaw a kind of crisis for this period. Externally this crisis arose because these years in particular were the hey-day of the so called liberal ideas. In the forties it seemed as if the impulse of the Consciousness Soul in the form of liberalism might breach the walls of reactionary conservatism in Europe. Two things concurred in these years. The proletariat was still the prisoner of its historical origins, it lacked self-assurance, confidence in itself. Only in the sixties was it ready to play a conscious part in historical evolution; before this one cannot speak of proletarian consciousness in the modern sense of the term. The social question of course existed before the sixties, but the middle class was totally unaware of it. At the end of the sixties an Austrian minister[1] of repute made the famous remark: 'The social question ends at Bodenbach!' Bodenbach, as you perhaps know, lies on the frontier between Saxony and Austria. Such was the famous dictum of a bourgeois minister!

In the forties therefore the proletarian consciousness did not yet exist. In the main, the bearer of the political life at that time was the bourgeoisie. Now the ideas which could have become a political force in the 1840's were exceedingly abstract. You are all familiar (at least to a certain extent I hope) with what are called the revolutionary ideas—in reality they were liberal ideas—which swept over Europe in the forties and unleashed the storm of 1848. As you know, the bearer of these ideas was the middle class. But all these ideas which were prevalent at the time and which were struggling to find a place in the historical evolution of mankind were totally abstract, sometimes merely empty words! But there was no harm in that, for in the epoch of the

Consciousness Soul one had to go through the abstractive phase and apprehend the leading ideas of mankind first of all in this abstract form.

Now you know from your own experience and that of others that the human being does not learn to read or write overnight. In order to develop certain potentialities mankind also needs time to prepare the ground. And mankind was given until the end of the seventies to develop new ideas. Let us look at this a little more closely. Starting from the year 1845, add thirty-three years and we arrive at the year 1878. Up to this year, approximately, mankind was given the opportunity of becoming acclimatized to the reality of the ideas of the forties. The decades between the forties and the seventies are most important for an understanding of modern evolution, for it was in the forties that what are called liberal ideas, albeit in an abstract form, began to take root and mankind was given until the end of the seventies to apprehend those ideas and relate them to the realities of the time.

But the bearer of these ideas, the bourgeoisie, missed their opportunity. The evolution of the nineteenth century is fraught with tragedy. For those who listened to the speeches of the outstanding personalities of the bourgeoisie in the forties (and there were many such throughout the whole civilized world) announcing their programme for a radical change in every sphere, the forties and fifties seemed to herald the dawn of a new age. But, owing to the characteristics of the middle class which I have already described, hopes were dashed. By the end of the seventies the bourgeoisie had failed to grasp the import of liberal ideas. From the forties to the seventies the middle class had been asleep and we cannot afford to ignore the consequence. The tide of events is subject to a pattern of ebb and flow and mankind can only look forward to a favourable development in the

## Lecture IV

future if we are prepared to face frankly what occurred in the immediate past. We can only wake up in the epoch of the Consciousness Soul if we are aware that we have hitherto been asleep! If we are unaware when and how long we have been asleep, we shall not awake up, but continue to sleep on.

When the Archangel Michael took over his task as Time Spirit at the end of the seventies the bourgeoisie had not understood the political impact of liberal ideas. The powers which in this epoch intervened in the life of mankind began by obscuring the nature of these ideas. And if you take the trouble, you can follow this very clearly. How different was the configuration of the political life at the end of the nineteenth century from that envisaged in the forties! One cannot imagine a greater contrast than the ideas of 1840–1848 (which were certainly abstract, yet lucid despite their abstract nature), and the 'lofty human ideals', as they were called, in the different countries in the nineteenth century and even up to our own time, when they ended in catastrophe.

The temporal complement therefore to the spatial picture is this: in the most productive and fertile years for the bourgeoisie, from the forties to the end of the seventies, they had been asleep. Afterwards it was too late, for nothing could then be achieved by following the path along which the liberal ideal might have been realised in this period. Afterwards only through conscious experience of spiritual realities could anything be achieved. There we see the connection between historical events.

In the period between the forties and the seventies the ideas of liberalism, though abstract, were such that they tended to promote tolerance between men. And assuming for the moment that these ideas were realized, then we should see the beginning, only the first steps it is true, but

*From Symptom to Reality in Modern History*

nonetheless a beginning of a tolerant attitude towards others, a respect for their ideas and sentiments which is so conspicuously lacking today. And so in social life a far more radical, a far more powerful idea, an idea which has its source in the spirit, must lay hold of men. I propose first of all, purely from the point of view of future history, to indicate this idea and will then substantiate it in greater detail.

Only a genuine concern of each man for his neighbour can bring salvation to mankind in the future—I mean to his community life. The characteristic feature of the epoch of the Consciousness Soul is man's isolation. That he is inwardly isolated from his neighbour is the consequence of individuality, of the development of personality. But this separative tendency must have a reciprocal pole and this counterpole must consist in the cultivation of an active concern of every man for his neighbour.

This awakening of an active concern for others must be developed ever more consciously in the epoch of the Consciousness Soul. Amongst the fundamental impulses indicated in my book *Knowledge of the Higher Worlds. How is it achieved?* you will find mentioned the impulse which, when applied to social life, aims at enhancing understanding for others. You will find frequent mention of 'positiveness', the need to develop a positive attitude. The majority of men today will certainly have to foreswear their present ways if they wish to develop this positive attitude, for at the moment they have not the slightest notion what it means. When they perceive something in their neighbour which displeases them —I do not mean something to which they have given careful consideration, but something which from a superficial angle meets with their disapproval—they immediately begin to criticize, without attempting to put themselves in their neighbour's skin. It is highly anti-social from the point of view of the future evolution of mankind—this may perhaps

## Lecture IV

seem paradoxical, but it is none the less true—to harbour these tendencies and to approach one's neighbour with undisguised sympathy or antipathy. On the other hand the finest and most important social attribute in the future will be the development of a scientific objective understanding of the shortcomings of others, when we are more interested in their shortcomings than in our concern to criticize them. For gradually in the course of the fifth, sixth and seventh cultural epochs the individual will have to devote himself increasingly and with loving care to the shortcomings of his neighbour. On the pediment of the famous temple of Apollo in Greece was inscribed this motto: 'Know thyself'. Self knowledge in the highest sense could still be achieved at that time through introspection. But that is becoming progressively less possible. Today man has made little advance in self knowledge through introspection. Fundamentally men know so little of each other because they are concerned only with themselves, and because they pay so little attention to others, especially to what they call the shortcomings of others.

This can be confirmed by a purely scientific fact. Today when the scientist wants to discover the secrets of human, animal and plant life he does two things. I have often spoken of this and it is most important. First of all he carries out an experiment, following the same procedure for inorganic life as for organic life. But by experimentation he loses touch with living nature. He who is able to follow with true insight the results of experimentation knows that the experimental method is shot through with the forces of death. All that experimentation can offer, even the patient and painstaking work of Oskar Hertwig[2] for example, is dead-sea fruit. It cannot explain how a living being is fertilized, nor how it is born. By this method one can only explain the inorganic. The art of experimentation can tell us nothing of the secrets of life. That is the one side.

*From Symptom to Reality in Modern History*

Today however there is one field of investigation which operates with very inadequate means and is as yet in its very early stages, but which is calculated to give valuable information about human nature, namely, the study of pathological conditions in man. When we study the case history of a man who is not quite normal we feel that we can be at one with him, that with sympathetic understanding we can break through the barrier that separates us from him and so draw nearer to him. By experimentation we are detached from reality; by the study of what are called today pathological conditions—malformations as Goethe so aptly called them— we are brought back to reality. We must not be repelled by them, but must develop an understanding for them. We must say to ourselves: the tragic element in life—without ever wishing it for anybody—can sometimes be most instructive, it can throw a flood of light upon the deepest mysteries of life. We shall only understand the significance of the brain for the life of the soul through a more intensive study of the mentally disturbed. And this is the training ground for a sympathetic understanding of others. Life uses the crude instrument of sickness in order to awaken our interest in others. It is this concern for our neighbour which can promote the social progress of mankind in the immediate future, whereas the reverse of positiveness, a superficial attitude of sympathy or antipathy towards others makes for social regression. These things are all related to the mystery of the epoch of the Consciousness Soul.

In every epoch of history mankind develops some definite faculty and this faculty plays an important role in evolution. Recall my words at the end of the last lecture. I said: men must be prepared to recognize more and more in the events of external history creation and destruction, birth and death, birth through impregnation with a new spiritual revelation, death through everything that we create. For the

## Lecture IV

fundamental characteristic of the epoch of the Consciousness Soul is that, on the physical plane, we can only create if we are aware that everything we create is destined to perish. Death is inherent in everything we create. On the physical plane the most important achievements of recent time are fraught with death. And the mistake we make is not that our creations are fraught with death, but that we refuse to recognize that they are vehicles of death.

After the first fifth of the epoch of the Consciousness Soul has elapsed, people still say today: man is born and dies. They avoid saying, for it seems absurd: to what end is man born if he is destined to die? Why bring a man into the world when we know that death is his lot. In that event birth is meaningless! Now people do not say this, because nature in her wisdom compels them to accept birth and death in the sphere of external nature. In the sphere of history, however, they have not yet reached the stage when they accept birth and death as the natural order of things. Everything created in the domain of history, they believe, is without exception good and is destined to subsist for ever. In the epoch of the Consciousness Soul we must develop a sense that the external events of history are subject to birth and death, and that, whatever we create, be it a child's toy or an empire, we create in the knowledge that it must one day perish. Failure to recognize the impermanence of things is irrational, just as it would be irrational to believe that one could bear a child which was entitled to live on earth for ever.

In the epoch of the Consciousness Soul we must become fully aware that the works of man are impermanent. In the Graeco-Latin epoch this was not necessary, for at that time the course of history followed the natural cycle of birth and death. Civilizations rose and fell as a natural process. In the epoch of the Consciousness Soul it is man who weaves birth and death into the web of his social life. And in this epoch man can acquire a sense for this because in the Graeco-Latin epoch this seed had been implanted in him under quite specific circumstances.

For a man of the middle Graeco-Latin epoch the most important moment in his development was the early thirties. These years were to some extent the focal point of two forces which are active in every man. The forces which operate in the symptoms of birth are active throughout the whole period from birth to death; but their characteristic features are manifested at birth. Birth is only one significant symptom of the activity of these forces; and the other occasions when the same forces are active throughout the whole of physical life are less important. In the same way, the forces of death begin to act at the moment of birth and when man dies they are especially evident. These two polar forces, the forces of birth and the forces of death, always maintain a kind of balance. In the Graeco-Latin epoch they were most evenly balanced when man reached the early thirties. Up to this age he developed his sentient life and afterwards, through his own efforts, his intellect. Before the thirties his intellectual life could only be awakened through teaching and education. And therefore we speak of the Graeco-Latin epoch as the era of the Rational or Intellectual Soul because the sentient life up to the age of thirty and the intellectual life which developed later were united. But this no longer applies in the epoch of the Consciousness Soul. Today intellectual development ceases before middle life. The majority of people one meets today, especially amongst the middle classes, do not mature after the age of twenty-seven; thereafter they are content to plough the same furrow. You can easily see what I mean by looking around you. How few people today have radically changed in any way since the age of twenty-seven. They have aged physically, their hair has turned grey, they have become decrepit . . . (perhaps that is going a little too far), but, on

## Lecture IV

the whole, man reckons that he has reached maximum potentiality by the age of twenty-seven. Let us take the case of a member of the so-called intellectual class. If he has had a sound training up to the age of twenty-seven he wants to establish himself; if he has gained a qualification he wants to make use of it and advance his career potential. Would you expect a man of average intelligence today to become a second Faust, that is to say, to study not only one faculty, but four faculties in succession up to the age of fifty? I do not mean that he should of necessity go to the university, perhaps there are better possibilities than the four faculties. A man who is prepared to continue his studies, to expand his knowledge, a man who remains plastic and capable of transformation is a rarity today. This was far more common amongst the Greeks, at least amongst the intellectual section of the population, because development did not cease in the early thirties. The forces inherited at birth were still very active. They began to encounter the forces leading to death; a state of equilibrium was established at the midway stage of life. Today this situation has come to an end; the majority hopes to be 'made' men, as the saying goes, by the age of twenty-seven. Yet at the end of their thirties they could recapture something of their youthful idealism and go forward to wider fields if they really wished to do so! But I wonder how many there are today who are prepared to make the readjustment necessary for the future evolution of mankind: to develop a constant readiness to learn, to remain plastic and to be ever receptive to change. This will not be possible without that active sympathy for others of which I have already spoken. Our hearts must be filled with a tender concern for our neighbour, with sympathetic understanding for his peculiarities. And precisely because this compassion and understanding must take hold of mankind it is so rarely found today.

## *From Symptom to Reality in Modern History*

What I have just described throws light upon an important fact of man's inner psychic development. The thread linking birth and death is broken to some extent between the ages of twenty-six to twenty-seven and thirty-seven to thirty-eight. In this decade of man's evolution the forces of birth and death are not fully in harmony. The disposition of soul which man needs, and which he could still experience in the Graeco-Latin epoch because the forces of birth and death were still naturally conjoined, this disposition of soul he must develop in the epoch of the Consciousness Soul because he is able to observe birth and death in the external life of history. In brief, our observation of external life must be such that we can face the world around us fearlessly and courageously, saying to ourselves: we must consciously create and destroy in all domains of life. It is impossible to create forms of social life that last for ever. He who works for social ends must have the courage constantly to build afresh, not to stagnate, because the works of man are impermanent and are doomed to perish, because new forms must replace the old.

Now in the fourth post-Atlantean epoch, the epoch of the Intellectual or Rational Soul, birth and death were active in man in characteristic fashion; as yet there was no need for him to be aware of them externally. Now, in the epoch of the Consciousness Soul he must perceive them externally; to this end he must again develop in himself something else, and this is very important.

Let us look at man schematically in relation to the fourth, fifth and sixth cultural epochs.

In the fourth post-Atlantean epoch (the Graeco-Latin epoch) man was conscious of birth and death when he looked within himself. Today he must first perceive the forces of birth and death externally, in the events of history, in order to discover them within himself. That is why it is so vitally

*Lecture IV*

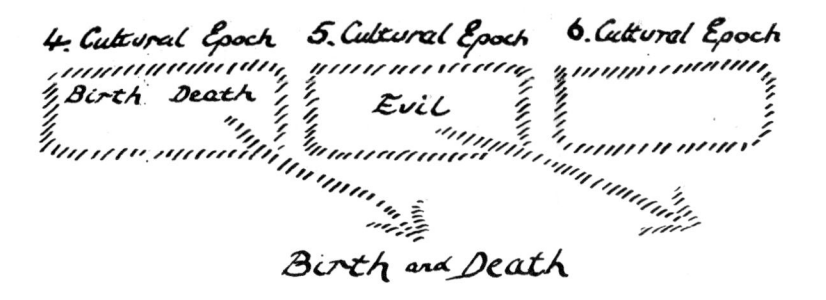

**4. Cultural Epoch** — Birth, Death
**5. Cultural Epoch** — Evil
**6. Cultural Epoch**

Birth and Death

important that in the epoch of the Consciousness Soul man should have a clear understanding of forces of birth and death in their true sense, i.e. a knowledge of repeated lives on earth, in order to acquire an understanding for birth and death in the unfolding of history.

But just as man's consciousness of birth and death has passed from an inner experience to an external realization, so in the fifth post-Atlantean epoch he must develop within himself something which in the sixth post-Atlantean epoch beginning in the fourth millennium will once again be experienced externally, namely, evil. In the fifth post-Atlantean epoch evil is destined to develop in man; it will ray outwards in the sixth epoch and be experienced externally— just as birth and death were experienced externally in the fifth epoch. Evil is destined to develop in man's inner being.

That is indeed an unpleasant truth! One can accept the fact that in the fourth post-Atlantean epoch man was familiar with birth and death as an inner experience and then perceived them in the cosmos as I pointed out in my lectures on the Immaculate Conception and the Resurrection, and the Mystery of Golgotha. Therefore mankind of the fourth post-Atlantean epoch is brought face to face with the phenomenon of the birth and death of Christ Jesus because birth and death were of vital importance in this epoch.

*From Symptom to Reality in Modern History*

Today when Christ is destined to appear again in the etheric body, when a kind of Mystery of Golgotha is to be experienced anew, evil will have a significance akin to that of birth and death for the fourth post-Atlantean epoch! In the fourth epoch the Christ impulse was born out of the forces of death for the salvation of mankind. We can say that we owe the new impulse that permeated mankind to the event on Golgotha. Thus by a strange paradox mankind is led to a renewed experience of the Mystery of Golgotha in the fifth epoch through the forces of evil. Through the experience of evil it will be possible for the Christ to appear again, just as He appeared in the fourth post-Atlantean epoch through the experience of death.

In order to understand this—we have already given here and there a few indications of the Mystery of Evil—we must now say a few words about the relationship between the Mystery of Evil and the Mystery of Golgotha. This relationship will be the subject of our next lecture.

## LECTURE V

Even within the limits enjoined upon us by discretion at the present time when one speaks of these matters, one cannot discuss the Mystery of Evil without profound emotion. For here we touch upon one of the deepest mysteries of the fifth post-Atlantean epoch, upon something which meets with little understanding today. Man's sensitivity to these things is but little developed as yet. Nonetheless, in all the so-called secret societies of recent times repeated attempts have been made to give certain indications, in the form of symbols, of the Mystery of Evil and the Mystery of Death which is related to it. But since the last third of the nineteenth century these symbolical representations have seldom been treated seriously, even in the Masonic communities, or have been treated in the manner I indicated here two years ago with reference to important events of the present day.*

The indications I gave on that occasion were not without a deeper motive, for he who understands these things knows what unplumbed depths of human nature we touch upon here. There is ample evidence that in reality the will to understand these things scarcely exists today. But the will to understand will assuredly come with time and we must ensure by every means at our command that it is awakened. When speaking of these matters one must sometimes give the impression of wanting to criticize certain aspects of the contemporary scene. Even what I said yesterday, for example on the subject of the ideological aspirations of the bourgeoisie

* *Kosmische und menschliche Geschichte,* Vol II and Vol III (Bibl. Nrs. 171 and 172).

since the last third of the nineteenth century can also be regarded as a criticism if taken superficially. Nothing of what is said here is intended as a criticism; I simply wish to characterize, so that we are aware of what forces and impulses have been operative. From a certain point of view it was necessary that these impulses should predominate. One could show that it was a historical necessity that the bourgeoisie of Europe should remain asleep from the forties to the end of the seventies. Nonetheless the knowledge of this 'cultural sleep' ought to have a positive effect; it ought to awaken today certain impulses of cognition and volition which will prepare the ground for the future.

In the present epoch of the Consciousness Soul two mysteries (as I have already indicated, I can only speak of them within certain limits) are of particular importance for the evolution of mankind—the Mystery of Death and the Mystery of Evil. From a certain angle the Mystery of Death which is related to the Mystery of Evil during the present epoch, immediately raises the vital question: what is the meaning of death for human evolution?

I recently said once again that what passes for science today takes the line of least resistance in these questions. For most scientists death is simply cessation of life, irrespective of whether it is the death of a plant, animal or human being. Spiritual science however cannot take the easy road by treating everything alike. Otherwise the death of a man could be equated with the end of a watch, the death of a watch. For man death is something totally different from the so-called death of other beings. We can only understand the phenomenon of death against the background of those forces which are operative in the universe and which, when they lay hold of man, are responsible for his physical death. Certain forces, certain impulses are active in the universe: but for them man could not suffer death. Man is part of the

## Lecture V

universe; these forces also permeate man and when they are active in man they cause his death. The question now arises; what do these forces which are active in the universe accomlish apart from bringing death to man? It would be a mistake to imagine that their sole purpose is to bring death to man; that is only a secondary effect. It would never occur to anyone to say: the function of a railway engine is to wear down the rails. Yet that is what actually happens; the engine gradually wears down the rails, it cannot do otherwise. But that is not its function—it is designed for a different purpose. If one were to define a locomotive as a machine whose function is to wear down the rails, one would obviously be talking nonsense. Nonetheless there is no denying the fact that there is a connection between the wearing down of the track and the nature of the locomotive. It would be equally mistaken to say that the forces in the universe which bring death to man exist for this sole purpose. This is only a secondary effect. Their real function is to endow man with the capacity to develop the Consciousness Soul. You see how close is the connection between the Mystery of Death and the evolution of the fifth post-Atlantean epoch, and how important it is that in this fifth post-Atlantean epoch the Mystery of Death should be revealed to all. For the task of the forces which as a secondary effect bring death to man is to implant in him, in the course of his evolution, not the Consciousness Soul, but the capacity to develop the Consciousness Soul.

This leads not only to an understanding of the Mystery of Death, but also encourages us to think precisely in matters of importance. In many respects modern thinking—and again this is not intended as a criticism, I merely wish to characterize—is, if I may use the familiar expression which is much to the point, simply 'sloppy' (schlampig). The thinking current in modern science is almost without exception typical of the kind of thinking that says: the function of the locomotive is to wear down the rails. Most scientific pronouncements today are on this level. Such thinking will prove to be inadequate if we wish to create in the future a state of affairs beneficial to mankind. And in the epoch of the Consciousness Soul this can only be achieved in full consciousness.

I must constantly remind you that this is a truth of profound importance for our time. We frequently hear of people who, drawing upon a seeming fund of wisdom, suggest various social and economic measures, in the belief that it is still possible today to make these recommendations without the help of spiritual science. Only those who think in contemporary terms, in conformity with the needs of the time, realize that all proposals for a future structure of society which are not grounded in spiritual science are a snare and delusion. Only those who are fully aware of this think in conformity with the needs of the time. Those who still listen to the various learned discourses on political economy which are devoid of spiritual content are asleep to the demands of our time.

These forces, which must be described as the forces of death, took possession of man's corporeal nature in earlier times—how, you will find in my book *Occult Science*. They first penetrated into his soul life at that time. For the remainder of his earth evolution man must assimilate these forces of death, and in the course of the present epoch their influence upon him will be such that he brings to full expression in himself the faculty of the Consciousness Soul.

The method I adopted when enquiring into the Mystery of Death, i.e. into the forces which are active in the universe and bring death to man, is equally valid for indicating the forces of evil. Even the forces of evil are not designed to promote evil actions within the human order—that again is only a secondary effect. If these forces did not exist in the

## Lecture V

universe man could not develop the Consciousness Soul; he would be unable to receive as he should in the course of his future evolution the forces of the Spirit Self, the Life Spirit and the Spirit Man. He must first pass through the stage of the Consciousness Soul if he wishes to receive after his own fashion the forces of the Spirit Self, the Life Spirit and the Spirit Man. And to this end he must, in the course of the fifth post-Atlantean epoch, i.e. up to the middle of the fourth millennium, fully unite his being with the forces of death. This lies within his power. But he cannot unite his own being with the forces of evil in the same way. The forces of evil in the cosmos are such that only in the Jupiter epoch will he be able to assimilate them as he now assimilates the forces of death. One can say therefore that the forces of evil act upon man with less intensity, they take possession of only a part of his being. In order to understand the nature of these forces of evil we must not look to their external effects, but must look for evil where it reveals its true nature, where it acts as it must of necessity act, because the forces which appear as evil in the universe also play into man. And here we touch upon something that can be spoken of only with deep emotion, something we can only express if we assume at the same time that it will be received with the greatest seriousness. If we wish to enquire into evil in man we must not look for it in the evil actions of society, but in evil tendencies. We must first of all ignore completely the consequences of these tendencies which are manifested more or less in a particular individual and turn our attention to the evil tendencies themselves. The question then arises: in which men are evil tendencies active in our present fifth post-Atlantean epoch, those tendencies which, in their secondary effects, are so clearly manifested in evil actions? Which men are subject to these evil tendencies?

## From Symptom to Reality in Modern History

We receive the answer to our question when we attempt to cross what is called the 'threshold of the Guardian' and to acquire a real understanding of the being of man. And the answer is this: since the beginning of the fifth post-Atlantean epoch, evil tendencies are subconsciously present in *all* men. It is precisely this influx of evil tendencies into men that marks his entrance into the fifth post-Atlantean epoch. Expressed somewhat radically one could say with every justification: he who crosses the threshold of the spiritual world discovers that there is not a crime in the calendar to which every man, in so far as he belongs to the fifth post-Atlantean epoch, is not subconsciously prone. Whether in a particular case this tendency leads to an evil action depends upon wholly different circumstances and not upon the tendency itself. If we are to tell mankind the plain unvarnished truth today, we cannot escape unpalatable facts.

The pressing question then arises: what is the purpose of these forces which induce evil tendencies in man, what is the purpose of these forces in the universe when they first infiltrate man's being? They are certainly not present in the universe in order to provoke evil acts in human society. (The reason why they promote evil acts will be discussed later.) These forces of evil do not exist in the universe for the sole purpose of inducing man to commit criminal acts any more than the forces of death exist simply to bring death to man; their function is to awaken in man, when he is called upon to develop the Consciousness Soul, the tendency to open himself to the life of the spirit, as I described yesterday.

Man must assimilate these forces of evil which are operative in the universe. By so doing he implants in his being the seed which enables him to experience consciously the life of the spirit. The purpose of these forces of evil which are perverted by the social order is to enable man to break through to the life of the spirit at the level of the Conscious-

## Lecture V

ness Soul. If he did not open himself to these tendencies to evil he would not succeed in developing consciously the impulse to receive from the universe the spirit which henceforth must fertilize the whole sphere of cultural life if it is not to perish. Our best course is to consider first of all what is to become of those forces of which the evil actions of men are a caricature and to ask ourselves what is destined to happen in the course of the evolution of mankind under the influence of these forces which, at the same time, are the source of evil tendencies.

When one speaks of these things one must touch upon the very core of human evolution. At the same time they are related to the calamities that have overtaken mankind at the present time and will still befall it. For those disasters, like flashes of summer lightning, are harbingers of quite other things that are destined to overtake mankind—lightning flashes that today often reveal the reverse of what is destined to happen. These observations are not a reason for pessimism, but rather should serve to arouse us and stimulate us to action.

Perhaps we shall best achieve our purpose if we start from a concrete phenomenon. I spoke yesterday of an important impulse in the epoch of the Consciousness Soul—the development of an active concern on the part of every man for his neighbour. This mutual concern for each other must grow and develop in the course of man's subsequent evolution on earth, especially in four domains. First, as man prepares his future development, he will see his fellow man in a progressively different light. Today, when a little over a fifth of the epoch of the Consciousness Soul has run its course, man still shows little inclination to see his fellow man as he will have to learn to see him in the course of the epoch of the Consciousness Soul, up to the fourth millennium. Men still ignore the most important element in others, they have no real understanding of their neighbour. In this connection they have not taken full advantage of what art has implanted in their souls in the course of their different incarnations. Much can be learned by studying the development of art and on different occasions I have given many an indication of what can be learned from the evolution of art. If one observes the symptoms, as I have urged in these lectures, it is undeniable that in almost every branch of art artistic creation and appreciation are at a low ebb. Everything that has been undertaken in the field of art in recent decades clearly demonstrates that art is passing through a period of decadence. The most important contribution of art to the evolution of mankind is the training it provides for an understanding of future problems.

Every branch of culture, of course, has many ramifications and consequently all kinds of secondary effects, but art by its very nature embodies something that leads to a deeper and more concrete understanding of man. He who makes a thorough study of the artistic forms in painting and sculpture, or of the nature of the inner rhythms in music and poetry—and the artists themselves often fail to do this today—he who has a deep inner experience of art is imbued with something which enables him to understand the human being in his picture-nature. In the epoch of the Consciousness Soul mankind must develop the capacity to comprehend man symbolically. You are already familiar with some of the basic principles of this symbolical understanding. When we look at the human head we are reminded of man's earliest beginnings. Just as a dream is seen as a memory of the sensible world and thereby receives its characteristic stamp, so for those who understand reality everything pertaining to the sensible world is an image of the spiritual. We must learn to perceive the spiritual archetype of man through his picture-nature. In future man will become to some extent

## Lecture V

transparent to his fellow man. The form of his head, his gait, will awaken in us an inner sympathy and understanding of a different nature from what we find in human tendencies today. For we shall only know man as an ego-being when we have this conception of his picture-nature, when we can approach him with the fundamental feeling that what the physical eyes perceive of man bears the same relation to the true supersensible reality of man as the picture painted on canvas bears to the reality which it depicts. We must develop this fundamental feeling in ourselves. We must approach man in such a way that we no longer see him as a combination of bones, muscles, blood, etcetera, but as the image of his eternal, spiritual being. Supposing a man walks past us; we would not recognize him if he did not awaken in us the realization of what he is as an eternal spiritual supersens'ble being. This is how we shall see man and this is how we shall be able to see him in the future. When we perceive human forms and movements and all that is associated with them as an image of the eternal, we shall feel warmth or coldness and of necessity will gradually be filled with inner warmth or coldness. As we go through life we shall come to know man very intimately; towards some we shall feel warm, towards others cold. Worst of all will be the situation of those who evoke neither warmth nor coldness. We shall have an inner experience of others in the warmth ether that penetrates our etheric body; this will be the reaction of the enhanced interest that must be developed between men.

 A second factor must provoke even more paradoxical emotions in contemporary man who has not the slightest desire to accept these new ideas. But perhaps in the not too far distant future this antipathy will be transformed into sympathy for the right understanding of man. This second phase of future development will bring a totally different

## From Symptom to Reality in Modern History

understanding between men. In order to achieve this the two millennia from now until the end of the fifth post-Atlantean epoch will not suffice; a longer period will be necessary, reaching into the sixth epoch. Then, to the knowledge of the ego will be added a special capacity, the capacity to feel, to sense in our neighbour when we approach him his relationship to the third Hierarchy, to the angels, archangels and archai. And this will be developed through an increasing recognition that man's response to language will be different from that of the present day. The evolution of language has already passed its zenith. In reality language has already become abstract.* At the present time a wave of profound untruthfulness is sweeping over the world in that attempts are being made to create institutions on a linguistic basis. Men no longer have the relationship to language which reveals through language the being of man.

I have quoted on various occasions an example which may serve as a first step towards an understanding of this matter.† I cited it again in a public lecture which I gave in Zürich because it is important to draw the attention of the public to these things. I pointed out in this lecture that a surprise awaits us when we compare the articles of Herman Grimm on the methodology of history (for he was a typical representative of Central European culture) with those of Woodrow Wilson. I carried out this comparative study most conscientiously and showed that it is possible to substitute certain passages of Woodrow Wilson for passages in Hermann Grimm, for the wording is almost identical. Equally one could exchange whole passages of Grimm on historical methodology for those of Wilson on the same subject. And

* See *Die Wissenschaft vom Werden des Menschen*, August–September, 1918 (Bibl. Nr. 183).

† 14th March, 1918, *Das geschichtliche Leben der Menschheit und seine Rätsel* (in Bibl. Nr. 67) and 30th March, 1918, *Anthroposophischer Lebensgaben* (in Bibl. Nr. 181).

## Lecture V

yet there is a radical difference between the two which we perceive when we read them without concern for the content (for the content as such, taken literally, will have increasingly less importance for mankind in the course of their future evolution). The difference is this: in Grimm, everything, even the passages with which one may not agree, are the fruit of personal endeavour; he has wrestled with them sentence by sentence, step by step. In Wilson everything seems to be prompted by his own inner daimon which subconsciously possesses him. What is important is the source, the origin of these writings: in the one case it is directly at the threshold of consciousness, in the other case in the daimonic promptings which find their way from the subconscious into consciousness . . . so that one can say: the writings of Wilson are in part the product of possession.

I quote this example in order to show you that it is no longer of significance today that the words should be identical. I always feel extremely sad when friends of our movement bring me articles of some pastor or professor and say: Do look at this, it sounds quite anthroposophical! Now in our present cultural epoch even a professor who dabbles in politics may well write things which, taken literally, of course are in keeping with the realities of our time. It is not the exact words that matter, but the region of the soul whence these things arise. It is important to discover behind the words their spiritual source. All that I have said here does not spring from a desire to lay down definite principles. It is the 'how' that matters. It is important that these words should be permeated by that force which derives directly from the spirit. He who finds a verbal similarity between the articles of the pastor or professor and what I have said here without feeling that my words spring from a spiritual source and are imbued with spiritual substance because they reflect the totality of the anthroposophical *Weltanschauung*, he who ignores this 'how', fails to understand me if he does not distinguish between modern opinions that smack of Anthroposophy and Anthroposophy itself.

It is of course not very pleasant to point to examples of this kind because the tendency today is often to take the opposite course. But when we speak in earnest, if our words are not intended simply as an anodyne, a kind of cultural soporific, it is a duty, it is a necessity even, not to shrink from selecting such examples, though they may be distasteful to many. For those who are in earnest about the future must be prepared to face the consequences for everyone if they ignore the fact that the world may be fated to have its organization determined by a half-baked American professor. It is not easy to speak of realities today because many are satisfied with the life of illusion. Nonetheless one speaks of realities in those spheres where it is absolutely necessary, and where it is important, or at least should be important, for man to hear of them.

Men must learn to see through words; they will have to acquire the capacity to grasp the gesture in language. Before this epoch, before this fourth millennium has run its course, men will have learnt to listen to one another differently from the way they do at the present moment; they will find in language an external expression of man's relation to the third Hierarchy, to the angels, archangels and archai, a means whereby he can attain to the supersensible, to the spirit.

And thus the soul of man will be heard through language and this will lead to a totally different community life. And a large part of the so-called forces of evil must be transformed so that it will be possible by listening to what a man says to hear the soul through the words. Then when the soul is heard through the words people will experience a peculiar sensation of colour and through this sensation of colour

## Lecture V

arising from language men of all nations will learn to understand one another. A particular sound will evoke the same sensation as the perception of the colour blue or of a blue surface. Another sound will evoke the same sensation as the perception of the colour red. The normal sensation of warmth we feel when we look at a man becomes to some extent colour when we listen to him. And we shall have to experience in ourselves what echoes from human lips to human ears on the wings of sounds. This will be experienced by man in the future.

Thirdly, men will experience inwardly the emotional reactions of others. In this respect language will play an important role—and not only language. When one man confronts another he will experience in his own respiration the emotional configuration of the other. In future time respiration will adapt itself to the affective life of the person who confronts us. In the presence of one man we shall breathe more rapidly, in the presence of another we shall breathe more slowly. According to the changing rhythm of our respiration we shall feel the kind of man with whom we are dealing. Think how the social life of the community will be cemented, how intimate corporate life will become! It will be a long time, no doubt, before this goal is achieved. It will take the whole of the sixth post-Atlantean epoch and the early years of the seventh epoch before respiration is adapted to the life of the soul. And in the seventh epoch, a part of what is now the fourth stage of development will be realized. That is, when men belong to a community of their own volition, they will have to 'digest' one another, if you will pardon this crude expression. When we are compelled to will this or that in common with another, or will to want it, we shall have inner experiences akin to those which we have in a primitive form today when we consume a certain food. In the sphere of will men will have to 'digest' one another, in the sphere of feeling to 'breathe' one another; in the sphere of understanding through language they will have to experience one another through sensations of colour. And men will come to know one another as ego-beings when they learn to see each other as they really are.

But all these forces will be more inward, more related to the life of the soul. They will be fully developed only in the course of the Jupiter, Venus and Vulcan epochs. The earth evolution of mankind already demands psychic and spiritual indications of this development. The present age with its strange and calamitous development is the revolt of mankind against what is destined to follow from these developments which I have just described. Because in future all particularist tendencies in society must be abandoned, mankind rebels, and the trivial doctrine of national self determination is noised abroad. What we are witnessing today is a revolt against the divinely ordered course of evolution, a struggle to resist the inevitable. We must be aware of these things if we are to lay a firm foundation for an understanding of the Mystery of Evil. For evil is often a secondary effect of the force that must intervene in human evolution. When a locomotive that has to cover a long distance strikes a bad section of the track, it destroys the rails and comes to a halt. In its evolution mankind is moving towards the goals I have described to you. And it is the task of the Consciousness Soul to recognize that mankind must press forward consciously to these goals. But the present lines are badly laid and it will be some time before better lines are in position, for often people proceed to replace the old lines by others which are not a whit better.

But, as you see, spiritual science has no wish to be pessimistic. It sets out to show man where he really stands in evolution today. But it demands nonetheless that, at least

## Lecture V

for certain solemn moments of recollection, he can renounce certain current tendencies. And because men find it so difficult to make this sacrifice, because, in spite of everything, everyone immediately reverts to his old routine, it is extremely difficult to speak frankly on these matters today. For we touch upon here—and this is characteristic of our time—problems of the nature of evil which threaten to destroy mankind today and one must constantly exhort men to wake up.

Indeed, many things can only be discussed within certain limits and in consequence much will be omitted entirely or deferred to another occasion. Let us take an example that concerns us closely and do not take it amiss if I present it in the following way. A week ago I was asked to say something on the subject of the symptomatology of Swiss history. I have given the matter most careful thought from every angle. But if I, as a foreigner, were to embark upon the symptomatology of Swiss history from the fifteenth century until the present day in the presence of Swiss nationals here in Dornach, I would find myself in a very strange situation. Let me illustrate the problem from another angle. Suppose that in July of this year (1918) someone in Germany or even in Austria had described the events and personalities as people do today, imagine what an outburst there would have been if he had portrayed five, fifteen or thirty years ago, for example, the conditions in Austria today! I am aware, therefore, that I would cause grave offence if I were to speak of Swiss history as the Swiss will speak of it here in Switzerland twenty years hence. For people cannot do otherwise, given their innate conservatism, than close their ears to what must be said from the standpoint of the future. It is true that in many spheres ordinary people—and after all we must count ourselves amongst them—especially in spheres that touch them closely, are unwilling to hear the truth.

*From Symptom to Reality in Modern History*

They prefer an anodyne. I assure you that I would give offence if I did not temper to some extent the subject on which I have been asked to speak. In the light of further reflection I think it is best to leave matters alone for the present. For judgements which are passed now—and from which one would dissent to some extent—are reminders that, if we wish to portray certain events today, we should do as I did yesterday. When one criticizes the Russian revolution and when one describes the relationship of the bourgeoisie to the broad masses and to the more radical elements of the extreme left, any such criticism is regarded here in Switzerland as relatively harmless, as an edifying Sunday afternoon sermon and is tolerated. And then one can abandon oneself, I will not say to the illusion, but to the pious hope that what I have said will penetrate into a few souls and will prove more efficacious than the normal Sunday afternoon sermons . . . although even in matters of moment, the experience of recent years has often demonstrated the contrary. But to comment on the immediate situation is not the task of one, who not being a Swiss national, would speak to the Swiss of their own history. When I gave a general survey of recent history in a public lecture in Zürich\* I had of course to speak with a certain reserve, although I did not hesitate to indicate the radical consequences which must be drawn from the facts. It is extremely convenient for the majority of people today to look upon Woodrow Wilson as a great man, as a benefactor of mankind. But if one denies this and speaks the truth, the truth is found to be unpalatable and one is regarded as a mischief-maker! And this has always been the case with those truths which are drawn from the wellspring of the supersensible. But today we are living in the

\* *Die Geschichte der Neuzeit im Lichte geisteswissenschaftlicher Forschung,* 17th October, 1918 (included in Bibl. Nr. 73).

## Lecture V

epoch of the Consciousness Soul and it is necessary that mankind should be aware of certain truths.

There is really no point in continually repeating the obvious—that people today are not receptive to spiritual ideas. The question is not whether people are receptive or not, but whether we ourselves take the necessary steps in order to bring before mankind the necessary truths when the opportunity arises. And in addition we should harbour no illusions about the receptivity of mankind to truths. We must be quite clear that, today especially, men are seldom receptive to what is vitally necessary for them . . . and that they insist upon ordering the world in a way that does not correspond with the true evolutionary impulse of our epoch. Indeed one experiences the bitterest disappointments in this domain. But one accepts them without resentment, in order to learn from them what we are to do under certain circumstances.

I will speak later of these matters in greater detail. It would have been a splendid thing if only a few people could have been found in Central Europe who, from an understanding of certain Masonic impulses, could have realized the significance of what I said here two years ago on the subject of secret societies. But, inevitably, there was no response. One cannot imagine a more sterile attitude than that of Central European Masonry in recent decades. This is shown by the fact, frequently mentioned, that one meets with resistance when one refuses to amalgamate in any way the teachings of spiritual science with the Freemasonry of Central Europe. On the other hand when a super windbag, the so-called Nietzsche specialist, Horneffer,[1] appeared and talked solemn nonsense about symbolism and the like, he was taken seriously in many quarters. The deeper reason for all this is that certain demands are made upon those who wish to take up spiritual science, and this is by no means easy!

## From Symptom to Reality in Modern History

One finds today advocates of a renewal of the spirit who explain to people that they need only lie down on a couch and relax and the higher ego, God, and heaven knows what else will awaken in them and then there will be no need to wrestle with these terrible concepts of anthroposophically orientated spiritual science. One need only listen to one's inner voice, surrender passively, then the higher mystical ego will manifest itself and one will feel and experience the presence of God in oneself.

I have known statesmen who prefer to listen to these 'pundits' who recommend them to take the easy path to the higher ego rather than listen to the teachings of spiritual science. A friend told me recently that one of these pundits had said to him when he was still one of his disciples: you have no idea how stupid I am! Yet this very man who confessed to his stupidity in order to show that intelligence is not needed in order to introduce men to the primal sources of wisdom, this man has a large following everywhere. People prefer to listen to such men rather than to those who speak of the thorny path ahead if man is to understand the task of the Consciousness Soul, who tell us of four aspects of evolution or that men must experience one another through warmth, through a sensation of colour, through respiration, that they must 'digest' one another. In order to arrive at an understanding of this, one must swallow a whole library of books—a most unpleasant prospect! But people find this prospect unpalatable, most unpalatable! But if people find this prospect unpalatable, that is due to the impulse which is impelling our age towards catastrophe, to the tragedy of our time. This situation, however, is no cause for pessimism; rather is it a call to energetic action, to translate our knowledge into deeds. And this cannot be repeated too often.

I mentioned yesterday the problem of suction and pressure in connection with the Russian revolution. I leave it to

## Lecture V

each of you to ask yourselves if this problem after all is not a matter deserving of careful reflection. Otherwise people might say: It is true that in Russia the bourgeoisie failed to unite with the peasants, but here in Germany we are more fortunate, bourgeoisie and peasants will join forces and then socialism will come into its own. But they forget that many people in Russia said the same and it is precisely because people held this view that Russia collapsed.

We will continue our discussion tomorrow.

## LECTURE VI

I have spoken to you from various points of view of the impulses at work in the fifth post-Atlantean epoch. You suspect—for I could only draw your attention to a few of these impulses—that there are many others which one can attempt to lay hold of in order to comprehend the course of evolution in our epoch. In my next lectures I propose to speak of the impulses which have been active in the civilized world since the fifteenth century, especially the religious impulses. I will attempt therefore in the three following lectures to give you a kind of history of religions.

Today I should like to discuss briefly something which some of you perhaps might find superfluous, but which I am anxious to discuss because it could also be important in one way or another for those who are personally involved in the impulses of the present epoch. I should like to take as my starting point the fact that at a certain moment, I felt that it was necessary to lay hold of the impulses of the present time in the ideas which I put forward in my book *The Philosophy of Freedom.*

The book appeared, as you know, a quarter of a century ago and has just been reprinted. I wrote *The Philosophy of Freedom*—fully conscious of the exigencies of the time—in the early nineties of the last century. Those who have read the preface which I wrote in 1894 will feel that I was animated by the desire to reflect the needs of the time. In the revised edition of 1918 I placed the original preface of 1894 at the end of the book as a second appendix. Inevitably when a book is re-edited after a quarter of a century circumstances

## Lecture VI

have changed; but for certain reasons I did not wish to suppress anything that could be found in the first edition.

As a kind of motto to *The Philosophy of Freedom* I wrote in the original preface: 'Truth alone can give us assurance in developing our individual powers. Whoever is tormented by doubts finds his powers emasculated. In a world that is an enigma to him he can find no goal for his creative energies.' 'This book does not claim to point the only possible way to truth, it seeks to describe the path taken by one who sets store upon the truth.'

I had been only a short time in Weimar when I began to write *The Philosophy of Freedom*. For some years I had carried the main outlines in my head. In all I spent seven years in Weimar. The complete plan of my book can be found in the last chapter of my doctoral dissertation, *Truth and Science*. But in the text which I presented for my doctorate I omitted of course this last chapter.

The fundamental idea of *The Philosophy of Freedom* had taken shape when I was studying Goethe's *Weltanschauung* which had occupied my attention for many years. As a result of my Goethe studies and my publications on the subject of Goethe's *Weltanschauung* I was invited to come to Weimar and collaborate in editing the Weimar edition of Goethe's works, the Grand Duchess Sophie edition as it was called. The Goethe archives founded by the Grand Duchess began publication at the end of the eighties.

You will forgive me if I mention a few personal details, for, as I have said, I should like to describe my personal involvement in the impulses of the fifth post-Atlantean epoch. In the nineties of the last century in Weimar one could observe the interweaving of two streams—the healthy traditions of a mature, impressive and rich culture associated with what I should like to call Goetheanism, and the traditional Goetheanism in Weimar which at that time was coloured by the heritage of Liszt. And also making its influence felt—since Weimar through its academy of art has always been an art centre—was what might well have provided important impulses of a far-reaching nature if it had not been submerged by something else. For the old, what belongs to the past, can only continue to develop fruitfully if it is permeated and fertilized by the new. Alongside the Goetheanism—which survived in a somewhat petrified form in the Goethe archives, (but that was of no consequence, it could be rejuvenated, and personally I always saw it as a living force)—a modern spirit invaded the sphere of art. The painters living in Weimar were all influenced by modern trends. In those with whom I was closely associated one could observe the profound influence of the new artistic impulse represented by Count Leopold von Kalkreuth[1] who at that time, for all too brief a period, had been a powerful seminal force in the artistic life of Weimar. In the Weimar theatre also a sound and excellent tradition still survived, though marred occasionally by philistinism. Weimer was a centre, a focal point where many and various cultural streams could meet.

In addition, there was the activity of the Goethe archives which were later enlarged and became the Goethe-Schiller archives. In spite of the dry philological approach which lies at the root of the work of archives, and reflects the spirit of the time and especially of the outlook of Scherer,[2] an active interest on the more positive impulses of the modern epoch was apparent, because the Goethe archives became the magnet for international scholars of repute. They came from Russia, Norway, Holland, Italy, England, France and America and though many did not escape the philistinism of the age it was possible nonetheless to detect amongst this gathering of international scholars in Weimar, especially in the nineties, signs of more positive forces. I still vividly recall

## Lecture VI

the eccentric behaviour of an American professor* who was engaged on a detailed study of *Faust*. I still see him sitting crosslegged on the floor because he found it convenient to sit next to the bookshelf where he could immediately put his hand on the reference books he needed without having to return continually to his chair. I remember also the gruff Treitschke[3] whom I once met at lunch and who wanted to know where I came from. (Since he was deaf one had to write everything down on slips of paper.) When I replied that I came from Austria he promptly retorted, characterizing the Austrians in his inimitable fashion: well, the Austrians are either extremely clever people or scoundrels! And so one could take one's choice; one could opt for the one or the other. I could quote you countless examples of the influence of the international element upon the activities in Weimar.

One also learned much from the fact that people also came to Weimar in order to see what had survived of the Goethe era. Other visitors came to Weimar who excited a lively interest for the way in which they approached Goetheanism, etcetera. I need only mention Richard Strauss[4] who first made his name in Weimar and whose compositions deteriorated rather than improved with time. But at that time he belonged to those elements who provided a delightful introduction to the modern trends in music. In his youth Richard Strauss was a man of many interests and I still recall with affection his frequent visits to the archives and the occasion when he unearthed one of the striking aphorisms to be found in Goethe's conversations with his contemporaries. The conversations have been edited by Waldemar Freiherr von Biedermann[5] and contain veritable pearls of wisdom. I mention these details in order to depict

* Thomas Calvin, Professor of Germanic Languages and Literatures at the University of Columbia.

135

the milieu of Weimar at that time in so far as I was associated with it.

A distinguished figure, a living embodiment of the best traditions of the classical age of Weimar, quite apart from his princely origin, was a frequent visitor to the archives. It was the Grand Duke Karl Alexander whose essentially human qualities inspired affection and respect. He was the survivor of a living tradition for he was born in 1818 and had therefore spent the fourteen years of his childhood and youth in Weimar as a contemporary of Goethe. He was a personality of extraordinary charm. And in addition to the Duke one had also the greatest admiration for the Grand Duchess Sophie of the house of Orange who made herself responsible for the posthumous works of Goethe and attended to all the details necessary for their preservation. That in later years a former finance minister was appointed head of the Goethe Society certainly did not meet with approval in Weimar. And I believe that a considerable number of those who were by no means philistine and who were associated in the days of Karl Alexander with what is called Goetheanism would have been delighted to learn, in jest of course, that perhaps after all there was something symptomatic in the Christian name of the former finance minister who became president of the Goethe Society. He rejoiced in the Christian name of Kreuzwendedich[6].

I wrote *The Philosophy of Freedom* when I was deeply involved in this milieu and I feel certain that it expressed a necessary impulse of our time. I say this, not out of presumption, but in order to characterize what I wanted to achieve and still wish to achieve with the publication of this book. I wrote *The Philosophy of Freedom* in order to give mankind a clear picture of the idea of freedom, of the impulse of freedom which must be the fundamental impulse of the fifth post-Atlantean epoch (and which must be developed

## Lecture VI

out of the other fragmentary impulses of various kinds.) To this end it was necessary first of all to establish the impulse of freedom on a firm scientific basis. Therefore the first section of the book was entitled 'Knowledge of Freedom'. Many, of course, have found this section somewhat repugnant and unpalatable, for they had to accept the idea that the impulse of freedom was firmly rooted in strictly scientific considerations based upon freedom of thought, and not in the tendency to scientific monism which is prevalent today. This section, 'Knowledge of Freedom', has perhaps a polemical character which is explained by the intellectual climate at that time. I had to deal with the philosophy of the nineteenth century and its *Weltanschauung*. I wanted to demonstrate that the concept of freedom is a universal concept, that only he can understand and truly feel what freedom is who perceives that the human soul is the scene not only of terrestrial forces, but that the whole cosmic process streams through the soul of man and can be apprehended in the soul of man. Only when man opens himself to this cosmic process, when he consciously experiences it in his inner life, when he recognizes that his inner life is of a cosmic nature will it be possible to arrive at a philosophy of freedom. He who follows the trend of modern scientific teaching and allows his thinking to be determined solely by sense perception cannot arrive at a philosophy of freedom. The tragedy of our time is that students in our universities are taught to harness their thinking only to the sensible world. In consequence we are involuntarily caught up in an age that is more or less helpless in face of ethical, social and political questions. For a thinking that is tied to the apron strings of sense perception alone will never be able to achieve inner freedom so that it can rise to the level of intuitions, to which it must rise if it is to play an active part in human affairs. The impulse of freedom has therefore been positively stifled by a thinking that is conditioned in this way.

The first thing that my contemporaries found unpalatable in my book *The Philosophy of Freedom* was this: they would have to be prepared first of all to fight their way through to a knowledge of freedom by self-disciplined thinking.

The second, longer section of the book deals with the reality of freedom. I was concerned to show how freedom must find expression in external life, how it can become a real driving force of human action and social life. I wanted to show how man can arrive at the stage where he feels that he really acts as a free being. And it seems to me that what I wrote twenty years ago could well be understood by mankind today in view of present circumstances.

What I had advocated first of all was an ethical individualism. I had to show that man can never become a free being unless his actions have their source in those ideas which are rooted in the intuitions of the single individual. This ethical individualism only recognized as the final goal of man's moral development what is called the free spirit which struggles free of the constraint of natural laws and the constraint of all conventional moral norms, which is confident that in an age when evil tendencies are increasing, man can, if he rises to intuitions, transmute these evil tendencies into that which, for the Consciousness Soul, is destined to become the principle of the good, that which is befitting the dignity of man. I wrote therefore at that time:

> Only the laws obtained in this way are related to human action as the laws of nature are related to a particular phenomenon. These laws however are in no way identical with the impulses which govern our actions. If we wish to understand how a man's action arises from his moral will, we must first study the relation of this will to the action.

I envisaged the idea of a free community life such as I described to you recently from a different angle—a free

## Lecture VI

community life in which not only the individual claims freedom for himself, but in which, through the reciprocal relationship of men in their social life, freedom as impulse of this life can be realized. And so I unhesitatingly wrote at that time:

> To live in love of our action and to let live in the full understanding of the other's will is the fundamental maxim of free men. They know no other obligation than that with which their will intuitively puts itself in harmony; how they will direct their will in a particular case will be determined by their capacity for ideas.

With this ethical individualism the whole Kantian school, of course, was ranged against me, for the preface to my essay *Truth and Science* opens with the words: 'We must go beyond Kant.' I wanted at that time to draw the attention of my contemporaries to Goetheanism—the Goetheanism of the late nineteenth century however—through the medium of the so-called intellectuals, those who regarded themselves as the intellectual elite. I met with little success. And this is shown by the article* which I recently wrote in the *Reich* and especially by my relations to Eduard von Hartmann.[7] You can imagine the alarm of contemporaries who were gravitating towards total philistinism, when they read this sentence† : When Kant apostrophizes duty:

> 'Duty! thou sublime and mighty name, thou that dost embrace within thyself nothing pleasing, nothing ingratiating, but dost demand submission, thou that dost establish a law ... before which all inclinations are silent even though they secretly work against it,' then, out of the consciousness of the free spirit, man replies: 'Freedom! thou kindly and humane name, thou that dost embrace all that is morally pleasing, all that my human dignity most cherishes and that makest me the servant of nobody, that settest up no new law, but dost await what my moral love itself will recognize as law, because, in face of every law imposed upon it, it feels itself unfree ...'

---

\* *Luziferisches und Ahrimanisches in ihrem Verhältnis zum Menschen.*
† p. 143 of the 1964 edition of *The Philosophy of Freedom.*

Thus the underlying purpose of *The Philosophy of Freedom* was to seek freedom in the empirical, in lived experience, a freedom which at the same time should be established on a firm scientific foundation. Freedom is the only word which has a ring of immediate truth today. If freedom were understood in the sense I implied at that time, then everything that is said today about the world order would strike a totally different note. We speak today of all sorts of things—of peace founded on justice, of peace imposed by force and so on. But these are simply slogans because neither justice nor force bear any relationship to their original meaning. Today our idea of justice is completely confused. Freedom alone, if our contemporaries had accepted it, could have awakened in them fundamental impulses and brought them to an understanding of reality. If, instead of such slogans as peace founded on justice, or peace imposed by force, people would only speak of peace based on freedom, then this word would echo round the world and in this epoch of the Consciousness Soul might kindle in the hearts of men a sense of security. Of course in a certain sense this second, longer section had a polemical intention, for it was necessary to parry (in advance) the attacks which in the name of philistinism, cheap slogans and blind submission to authority could be launched against this conception of the free spirit.

Now although there were isolated individuals who sensed which way the wind was blowing in *The Philosophy of Freedom*, it was extremely difficult—in fact it was impossible—to find my contemporaries in any way receptive to its message. It is true—amongst isolated voices—that a critic of the time wrote in the *Frankfurter Zeitung*: 'clear and true, that is the motto that could be written on the first page of this book', but my contemporaries had little understanding of this clarity and truth.

Now this book appeared at a time when the Nietzsche

## Lecture VI

wave was sweeping over the civilized world—and though this had no influence on the contents, it was certainly not without effect upon the hope I cherished that the book might nonetheless be understood by a few contemporaries. I am referring to the first Nietzsche wave when people realized that Nietzsche's often unbalanced mind was the vehicle of mighty and important impulses of the age. And before Nietzsche's image had been distorted by people such as Count Kessler[8] and Nietzsche's sister, in conjunction with such men as the Berliner, Karl Breysig,[8] and the garrulous Horneffer, there was every hope that, after the ground had been prepared by Nietzsche, these ideas of freedom might find a certain public. This hope was dashed when, through the people mentioned above, Nietzsche became the victim of modern decadence, of literary pretentiousness and snobism—(I do not know what term to choose in order to make myself understood).

After having written *The Philosophy of Freedom* I had first of all to observe how things developed—I am not referring to the ideas contained in the book (for I knew that at first few copies had been sold), but to the impulses which had been the source of the ideas in *The Philosophy of Freedom*. I had the opportunity of studying this for a number of years from the vantage point of Weimar.

However, shortly after its publication, *The Philosophy of Freedom* found an audience, an audience whom many would now regard as lukewarm. It found limited support in the circles associated with the names of the American, Benjamin Tucker,[9] and the Scottish-German or German-Scott, John Henry Mackay.[9] In a world of increasing philistinism this was hardly a recommendation because these people were among the most radical champions of a social order based on freedom of the spirit and also because when patronized to some extent by these people, as happened for a time in the case of *The Philosophy of Freedom*, one at least earned the right to have not only *The Philosophy of Freedom,* but also some of my later publications banned by the Russian censor! The *Magazin für Literatur* which I edited in later years found its way into Russia, but, for this reason, most of its columns were blacked out. But the movement with which the Magazin was concerned and which was associated with the names of Benjamin Tucker and J. H. Mackay failed to make any impression amid the increasing philistinism of the age. In reality that period was not particularly propitious for an understanding of *The Philosophy of Freedom,* and for the time being I could safely let the matter drop. It seems to me that the time has now come when *The Philosophy of Freedom* must be republished, when, from widely different quarters voices will be heard which raise questions along the lines of *The Philosophy of Freedom.*

You may say, of course, that it would have been possible nonetheless to republish *The Philosophy of Freedom* during the intervening years. No doubt many impressions could have been sold over the years. But what really matters is not that my most important books should sell in large numbers, but that they are understood, and that the spiritual impulse underlying them finds an echo in men's hearts.

In 1897 I left the Weimar milieu where I had been to some extent a spectator of the evolution of the time and moved to Berlin. After Neumann-Hofer had disposed of the *Magazin* I acquired it in order to have a platform for ideas which I considered to be timely, in the true sense of the word, ideas which I could advocate publicly. Shortly after taking over the *Magazin,* however, my correspondence with J. H. Mackay was published and the professoriate who were the chief subscribers to the *Magazin* were far from pleased. I was criticized on all sides. 'What on earth is Steiner doing with our periodical,' they said, 'what is he up to?' The whole professoriate of Berlin University who had subscribed to the

*Lecture VI*

*Magazin* at that time, in so far as they were interested in philology or literature —the *Magazin* had been founded in 1832, the year of Goethe's death and amongst other things this was one of the reasons why the University professors had subscribed to the review—this professoriate gradually cancelled their subscriptions. I must admit that with the publication of the *Magazin* I had the happy knack of offending the readers—the readers and not the *Zeitgeist*.

In this context I should like to recall a small incident. Amongst the representatives of contemporary intellectual life who actively supported my work on behalf of Goetheanism was a university professor. I will mention only one fact ... those who know me will not accuse me of boasting when I say that this professor once said to me in the Russischer Hof in Weimar: 'Alas, in comparison with what you have written on Goethe, all our trivial comments on Goethe pale into insignificance.' I am relating a fact, and I do not see why under present circumstances these things should be passed over in silence. For after all the second half of the Goethean maxim remains true (the first half is not Goethean): vain self praise stinks, but people rarely take the trouble to find out how unjust criticism on the part of others smells.[10]

Now this professor was also a subscriber to the *Magazin*. You will remember the international storm raised by the Dreyfus affair[11] at that time. Not only had I published in the *Magazin** information on the Dreyfus case that I alone was in a position to give, but I had vigorously defended† the famous article, *J'accuse*, which Zola had written in defence of Dreyfus. Thereupon I received from the professor who had sung my praises in divers letters (and even had these effusions printed) a postcard saying: 'I hereby cancel my subscription

* 11th December, 1897, *Die Instinkte der Franzosen* (see Bibl. Nr. 31).
† 19th February, 1898, *Emil Zola und die Jugend* (see Bibl. Nr. 31 for this and other articles).

to the *Magazin* once and for all since I cannot tolerate in my library a periodical that defends Emile Zola, a traitor to his country in Jewish pay.' That is only one little incident: I could mention hundreds of a similar kind. As editor of the *Magazin für Literatur* I was brought in contact with the dark corridors of the time and also with the modern trends in art and literature.\* Were I to speak of this you would have a picture of many characteristic features of the time.

Somewhat naively perhaps I had come to Berlin in order to observe how ideas for the future might be received by a limited few thanks to the platform provided by the *Magazin*—at least as long as the material resources available to the periodical sufficed, and as long as the reputation which it formerly enjoyed persisted, a reputation which, I must confess, I undermined completely. But I was able in all innocence to observe how these ideas spread amongst that section of the population which based its *Weltanschauung* upon the writings of that pot-house philistine Wilhelm Bölsche[12] and similar popular idols. And I was able to make extremely interesting studies which, from many and various points of view, threw light upon what is, and what is not, the true task of our epoch.

Through my friendship with Otto Erich Hartleben[13] I met at that time many of the rising generation of young writers who are now for the most part outmoded. Whether or not I fitted into this literary group is not for me to decide. One of the members of this group had recently written an article in the *Vossische Zeitung* which he tried to show in his pedantic way that I did not fit into this community and he looked upon me as an unpaid peripatetic theologian amongst a group of people who were anything but unpaid peripatetic theologians, but who were at least youthful idealists.

\* See *Die Veröffentlichungen aus dem literarischen Frühwerk R. Steiners*, Heft V, VIII, IX.

## Lecture VI

Perhaps the following episode will also interest you because it shows how I became for a time a devoted friend of Otto Erich Hartleben. It was during the time when I was still in Weimar. He always visited Weimar to attend the meetings of the Goethe Society; but he regularly missed them because it was his normal habit to get up at 2 in the afternoon and the meetings began at 10 a.m. When the meetings were over I used to call on him and usually found him in bed. Occasionally we would while away an evening together. His peculiar devotion to me lasted until the sensational Nietzsche affair in which I was involved severed our friendship. We were sitting together one evening and I recall how he warmed to me when, in the middle of the conversation, I made the epigrammatic remark: 'Schopenhauer is simply a narrow-minded genius.' Hartleben was delighted; and he was delighted with many other things I said the same evening so that Max Martersteig (who became famous in later years) jumped up at my remarks and said: 'Don't provoke me, don't provoke me.'

It was on one of the evenings which I spent in those days in the company of the promising Otto Erich Hartleben and the promising Max Martersteig and others that the first Serenissimus anecdote was born. It became the source of all later Serenissimus anecdotes. I should not like to leave this unmentioned; it certainly belongs to the milieu of *The Philosophy of Freedom*, for the spirit of *The Philosophy of Freedom* pervaded the circle I frequented and I still recall today the stimulus which Max Halbe[14] received from it (at least that is what he claimed). All these people had already read the book and many of the ideas of *The Philosophy of Freedom* have nonetheless found their way into the world of literature. The original Serenissimus anecdote from which all other Serenissimus anecdotes are derived did not by any means spring from a desire to ridicule a particular personality, but from

*From Symptom to Reality in Modern History*

that frame of mind that must also be associated with the impulse of *The Philosophy of Freedom*, namely, a certain humouristic attitude to life or—as I often say—an unsentimental view of life which is especially necessary when one looks at life from a deeply spiritual standpoint. This original anecdote is as follows:

His Serene Highness is visiting the state penitentiary and asks for a prisoner to be brought before him. The prisoner is brought in. His Highness then asks him a series of questions: 'How long have you been detained here?' 'Twenty years'— 'Twenty years! That's a good stretch. Tell me, my good fellow, what possessed you to take up your residence here?' 'I murdered my mother.' 'I see, you murdered your mother; strange, very strange! Now tell me, my good fellow, how long do you propose to stay here?' 'As long as I live; I have been given a life sentence.' 'Strange! That's a good stretch. Well, I won't take up your valuable time with further questions.' He turns to the prison Governor—'See that the last ten years of the prisoner's life sentence are remitted.'

That was the original anecdote. It did not spring from any malicious intention, but from a humorous acceptance of that which, if necessary, also has its ethical value. I am convinced that if the personality at whom this anecdote—perhaps mistakenly—was often directed had himself read this anecdote he would have laughed heartily.

I was able therefore to observe how in the Berlin circle I have mentioned attempts were made to introduce something of the new outlook. But ultimately a touch of the Bölsche crept into everything. I am referring of course not only to the fat Bölsche domiciled in Friedrichshagen, but to the whole Bölsche outlook which plays a major part in the philistinism of our time. Indeed the vulgarity of Bölsche's descriptions is eminently suited to the outlook of our time. When one reads Bölsche's articles one is compelled to handle ordure or the

## Lecture VI

like. And the same applies to his style. One need only pick up this or that article and we are invited to interest ourselves not only in the sexual life of the jelly fish, but in much else besides. This 'Bölsche-ism' has become a real tit-bit for the rising philistines in our midst today.

What I wrote one day in the *Magazin* was hardly the right way to launch it. Max Halbe's[14] drama, *Der Eroberer*, had just been performed. It certainly is a play with the best of intentions, but for that reason fell flat in Berlin. I wrote a criticism which reduced Halbe to sheer despair, for I took all the Berlin newspapers to task and told the Berlin critics one and all what I thought of them. That was hardly the way to launch the *Magazin*. But this was a valuable experience for me. Compared with the Weimer days one learned to look at many things from a different angle. But at the back of my mind there always lurked this question: how could the epoch be persuaded to accept the ideas of *The Philosophy of Freedom*? If you are prepared to take the trouble, you will find that everything I wrote for the *Magazin* is imbued with the spirit of *The Philosophy of Freedom*. However, the *Magazin* was not written for modern bourgeois philistines. But, of course, through these different influences I was gradually forced out.

At that very moment the opportunity of another platform presented itself—that of the socialist working class. In view of the momentous questions which were stirring the consciousness of the world at the turn of the century, questions with which I was closely associated through J. H. Mackay and Tucker who had come to Berlin from America and with whom I spent many an interesting evening, I was glad of this opportunity of another platform. For many years I was responsible for the curriculum in various fields at the Berlin school for workers' education. In addition I gave lectures in all kinds of associations of the socialist workers. I had been

## From Symptom to Reality in Modern History

invited not only to give these lectures, but also to conduct a course on how to debate. Not only were they interested in understanding clearly what I have discussed with you here in these lectures, but they were anxious to be able to speak in public as well, to be able to advocate what they deemed to be right and just. Exhaustive discussions were held on all sorts of topics and in widely different groups. And this again gave me an insight into the evolution of modern times from a different point of view. Now it is interesting to note that in these socialist circles one thing that is of capital importance for our epoch and for the understanding of this epoch was tabu. I could speak on any subject—for when one speaks factually one can speak today (leaving aside the proletarian prejudices) on any and every subject—save that of *freedom*. To speak of freedom seemed extremely dangerous. I had only a single follower who always supported me whenever I delivered my libertarian tirades, as the others were pleased to call them. It was the Pole, Siegfried Nacht. I do not know what has become of him—he always supported me in my defence of freedom against the totalitarian programme of socialism.

When we look at the present epoch and the new trends, we perceive that what is lacking is precisely what *The Philosophy of Freedom* seeks to achieve. On a basis of freedom of thought *The Philosophy of Freedom* establishes a science of freedom which is fully in accord with natural science, yet reaches beyond it. This section of the book makes it possible for really independent thinkers to be able to develop within the present social order. For if freedom without the solid foundation of a science of freedom were regarded as real freedom, then, in an age when evil is gaining ground (as I indicated yesterday), freedom would of necessity lead not to liberty, but to licence. What is necessary for the present epoch when freedom must become a reality can only be found in the firm inner discip-

## Lecture VI

line of a thinking freed from the tyranny of the senses, in genuine scientific thinking.

But socialism, the rising party of radicalism, which will assert itself even against the nationalists of all shades who are totally devoid of any understanding of their epoch, lacks any possibility of arriving at a science of freedom. For if there is one truth which is important for our epoch, it is this: socialism has freed itself from the prejudices of the old nobility, the old bourgeoisie and the old military caste. On the other hand it has succumbed all the more to a blind faith in the infallibility of scientific materialism, in positivism as it is taught today. This positivism (as I could show) is simply the continuation of the decree of the eighth Ecumenical Council of Constantinople in 869. Like an infallible and invisible pope this positivism holds in its iron grip the parties of the extreme left, including Bolshevism, and prevents them from attaining to freedom.

And that is the reason why, however much it seeks to assert itself, this socialism which is not rooted in the evolution of mankind, cannot do other than convulse the world for a long time, but can never conquer it. That is why it is not responsible for errors it has already committed and why others must bear the responsibility—those who have allowed it, or wished to allow it, to become not a problem of pressure, as I have shown,* but a problem of suction.

It is this inability to escape from the tentacles of positivism, of scientific materialism, which is the characteristic feature of the modern labour movement from the standpoint of those whose criterion is the evolution of mankind and not either the antiquated ideas of the bourgeoisie or what are often called new social ideas of Wilsonism, etcetera.

Now I have often mentioned that there would be no difficulty in introducing spiritual ideas to the working class.

* See Lecture IV.

But the leaders of the working class movement refuse to consider anything that is not rooted in Marxism. And so I was gradually pushed aside. I had attempted to introduce spiritual ideas and was to a certain extent successful, but I was gradually driven out.* One day I was defending spiritual values in a meeting attended by hundreds of my students and only four members who had been sent by the party executive to oppose me were present; nonetheless they made it impossible for me to continue. I still vividly recall my words: 'If people wish socialism to play a part in future evolution, then liberty of teaching and liberty of thought must be permitted.' Thereupon one of the stooges sent by the party leadership declared: 'In our party and its schools there can be no question of freedom, but only of reasonable constraint.' These things I may add are profoundly symptomatic of the forces at work today.

One must judge the epoch by its most significant symptoms. One must not imagine that the modern proletariat is not thirsting for spiritual nourishment! It has an insatiable craving for it. But the nourishment which it is offered is, in part, that in which it firmly believes, namely positivism, scientific materialism, or in part an indigestible pabulum that offers stones instead of bread.

*The Philosophy of Freedom* was bound to meet with opposition here, too, because its fundamental impulse, the impulse of freedom has no place in this most modern movement, (i.e. socialism).

Before this period had come to an end I was invited to give a lecture before the Berlin Theosophical Society. A series of lectures followed during the winter and this led to my association with the Theosophical movement. I have spoken of this in the preface to my book, *Die Mystik im*

* See Chapter XXVIII, *The Course of My Life*, Anthroposophic Press, New York, 1951.

## Lecture VI

*Aufgange des neuzeitlichen Geisteslebens und ihr Verhältnis zur modernen Weltanschauung.*\* I must emphasize once again—for this relationship with Theosophy has often been misunderstood—that at no time did I seek contact with the Theosophical Society; presumptuous as it may seem, it was the Theosophical Society which sought to make contact with me. When my book *Mysticism and Modern Thought* appeared not only were many chapters translated for the Theosophical Society, but Bertram Keightley and George Mead, who occupied prominent positions in the Society at the time, said to me: 'This book contains, correctly formulated, everything we have to elaborate.' At that time I had not read any of the publications of the Theosophical Society. I then read them, more or less as an 'official' only, although the prospect filled me with dismay.

But it was important to grasp the tendency of evolution, the impulse weaving and working in the life of the time. I had been invited to join the society; I could therefore join with good reason in accordance with my karma because I could perhaps find in the Theosophical Society a platform for what I had to say. I had of course to suffer much harassment. I should like to give an example which is symptomatic. One day when I attended a congress of the Theosophical Society for the first time I tried to put forward in a brief speech a certain point of view. It was at the time when the 'entente cordiale' had just been concluded and when everyone was deeply impressed by this event. I tried to show that in the movement which the Theosophical Society represents it is not a question of diffusing theosophical teachings from any random centre, but that the latest trends, the world over,

---

\* *Mysticism and Modern Thought*, Anthroposophical Publishing Co., London and Anthroposophic Press, New York, 1928 and as *Mysticism at the Dawn of the Modern Age*, Rudolf Steiner Publications, New Jersey, 1960.

should have a common meeting place, a kind of focal point. And I ended with these words: If we build upon the spirit, if we are really aiming to create a spiritual community in a concrete and positive fashion, so that the spirit which is manifested here and there is drawn towards a common centre, towards the Theosophical Society, then we shall build a different 'entente cordiale'.

It was my first speech before the Theosophical Society of London and I spoke intentionally of this entente cordiale. Mrs. Besant declared—it was her custom to add a few pompous remarks to everything that was said—that the 'German speaker' had spoken very beautifully. But I did not have the meeting on my side; and my words were drowned in the flood of verbiage that followed—whereas the sympathies of the audience and what they wanted was more on the side of the Buddhist dandy, Jinaradjadasa. At the time this too seemed to me symptomatic. After I had spoken of something of historical significance, of the other entente cordiale, I sat down and the Buddhist pandit, Jinaradjadasa, came tripping down from his seat higher up in the auditorium—and I say tripping advisedly in order to describe his movements accurately—tapping with his walking stick on the floor. His speech met with the approval of the audience, but at the time all that I remembered was a torrent of words.

I have emphasized from the very beginning—you need only read the preface to my book *Theosophy*—that the future development of theosophy will follow the lines of thought already initiated by *The Philosophy of Freedom*. Perhaps I have made it difficult for many of you to find an unbroken line of continuity between the impulses behind *The Philosophy of Freedom* and what I wrote in later years. People found the greatest difficulty in accepting as true and reliable what I attempted to say and what I attempted to have published. I had to suffer considerable provocation. In this society which I

## Lecture VI

had not sought to join, but which had invited me to become a member, I was not judged by what I had to offer, but by slogans and clichés. And this went on for some time until, at least amongst a small circle, I was no longer judged by slogans alone. Fundamentally, what I said or had published was relatively unimportant. It is true that people read it, but to read something does not mean that one has assimilated it. My books went through several editions, were reprinted again and again. But people judged them not by what I said or what they contained, but in terms of what they themselves understood, in the one case the mystical element, in another case the theosophical element, in a third case this, in a fourth case that, and out of this welter of conflicting opinions emerged what passed for criticism. Under the circumstances it was neither an ideal, nor an encouraging moment to have *The Philosophy of Freedom* reprinted. Although this book presents, of course in an incomplete, imperfect and infelicitous fashion, a small contribution to the fifth post-Atlantean epoch, nonetheless it seeks to express the fundamental, significant and really powerful impulses of this epoch.

Now that *The Philosophy of Freedom* has been republished after a quarter of a century I should like to emphasize that it is the fruit of a close and active participation in the life of the time, of an insight into our epoch, of the endeavour to detect, to apprehend what impulses are essential for our epoch. And now twenty-five years later, when the present catastrophe has overwhelmed mankind, I realize—you may perhaps attribute it to naivety—that this book is in the true sense of the word, timely; timely in the unexpected sense, that the contemporary world rejects the book *in toto* and often wants to know nothing of its contents.

If there had been any understanding of the purpose of this book—to lay the foundations of ethical individualism and of a social and political life—if people had really understood its purpose, then they would know that there exist today ways and means of directing human evolution into fertile channels—different from other paths—whilst the worst possible path that one could follow would be to inveigh against the revolutionary parties, to grumble perpetually and retail anecdotes about Bolshevism! It would be tragic if the bourgeoisie could not overcome their immediate concern for what the Bolsheviks have done here and there, for the way in which they behave towards certain people; for, in reality, that is beside the point. The real issue is to ascertain whether the demands formulated by the Bolsheviks are in any way justified. And if one can find a conception of the world and of life that dares to say that, if you follow the path indicated here, you will attain what you seek to achieve by your imperfect means, and much else besides—(and I am convinced that, if one is imbued with the Philosophy of Freedom, one dares to say that)—then light would dawn. And to this end the experience of a *Weltanschauung* founded on freedom is imperative. It is necessary to be able to grasp the fundamental idea of ethical individualism, to know that it is founded on the realization that man today is confronted with spiritual intuitions of cosmic events, that when he makes his own not the abstract ideas of Hegel, but the freedom of thought which I tried to express in popular form in my book *The Theory of Knowledge implicit in Goethe's World Conception*, he is actually in touch with cosmic impulses pulsating through the inner being of man.

Only through spiritual experiences is it possible to grasp the idea of freedom and to begin to regenerate those impulses which at the present time end in every case in a blind alley. The day when we realize that it is a waste of words to discuss such empty concepts as law, violence, etcetera, that the idea of freedom can only lead to reality when apprehended

## Lecture VI

through spiritual experiences, that day will herald a new dawn for mankind. To this end people must overcome their deep-seated apathy; they must abandon the practice, common amongst scientists today, of descanting on all kinds of social questions, on the various quack remedies for social and political amelioration. What they seek to achieve in this domain they must learn to establish on a firm, solid foundation of spiritual science. The idea of freedom must be anchored in a science of freedom.

It was evident to me that the proletariat is more receptive to a spiritual outlook than the bourgeoisie which is steeped in Bölsche-ism. One day for example after Rosa Luxemburg[15] had spoken in Spandau on 'science and the workers' before an audience of workers accompanied by their wives and children—the hall was full of screaming children, babes in arms and even dogs—I addressed the meeting. At first I intended to say only a few words, but finally my speech lasted one and a quarter hours. Taking up the thread of her theme I pointed out that a real basis already existed, namely, to apprehend science spiritually, i.e. to seek for new forms of life from out of the spirit. When I touched upon such questions I always found a measure of support. But hitherto everything has failed owing to the indolence of the learned professions, the scientists, doctors, lawyers, philosophers, teachers, etcetera on whom the workers ultimately depend for their knowledge. We met with all sorts of people—Hertzka[16] and his 'Freiland', Michael Flürscheim and many others who cherished ambitious social ideals. They all failed, as they were bound to fail, because their ideas lacked a spiritual basis, a basis of free, independent scientific thinking. Their ideas were the product of a thinking corrupted by its attachment to the sensible world such as one finds in modern positivism. The day that sees an end to the denial of the spirit, a denial that is characteristic of modern positivism, the day when we recognize that we must build upon a thinking freed from the tyranny of the senses, upon spiritual investigation, including all that is called science in the ethical, social and political domain, that day will mark the dawn of a new humanity. The day that no longer regards the ideas I have attempted to express here today, albeit so imperfectly, as the voice of one crying in the wilderness, but as ideas that will find their way to the hearts and souls of mankind today, that day will herald a new dawn! People listen to all sorts of things, even to Woodrow Wilson; they do more than listen to him. But that which is born of the spirit of human evolution finds little response in the hearts and souls of men. But a way must be found to evoke this response. Mankind must realize how the world would be transformed if the meaning of freedom were understood, freedom not in the sense of licence, but freedom born of a free spirit and a firmly disciplined mind. If people understood what freedom and its establishment would signify for the world, then the light which many seek today would lighten the prevailing darkness of our time.

This is what I wanted to say to you with reference to historical ideas. My time is up; there are many other things I wished to say, but they can wait for another occasion. I ask your indulgence for having included in my lecture many personal experiences of a symptomatic nature that I have undergone in my present incarnation. I wanted to show you that I have always endeavoured to treat objectively the things which concern me personally, to consider them as symptoms which reveal what the age and the spirit of the age demand of us.

## LECTURE VII

In the course of our enquiries during the next few days I should like to draw your attention to two things which seemingly bear little relation to each other. But when we have concluded our enquiries you will realize that they are closely connected. I should like in fact to touch upon certain matters which will provide points of view, symptomatic *points d'appui* concerning the development of religions in the course of the present fifth post-Atlantean epoch. And on the other hand, I would also like to show you in what respect the spiritual life that we wish to cultivate may be associated with the building which bears the name 'Goetheanum'.

It seems to me that the decisions taken in such a case have a certain importance, especially at the present time. We are now at a stage in the evolution of mankind when the future holds unknown possibilities and when it is important to face courageously an uncertain future and when it is also important, from out of the deepest impulses, to take decisions to which one attaches a certain significance. The external reason for choosing the name 'Goetheanum' seems to be this: I expressed the opinion a short time ago in public lectures that, for my part, I should like the centre for the cultivation of the spiritual orientation that I envisage to be called for preference the Goetheanum. The name to be decided upon had already been discussed last year; and this year a few of our members decided to support the choice of the name 'Goetheanum'. As I said recently there are many reasons for this choice, reasons which I find difficult to express in words. Perhaps they will become clear to you if I start today from considerations similar to those which I dealt with here last Sunday, by creating a basis for the study of the history of religions which we will undertake in these lectures.

You know of course—and I would not touch upon personal matters if they were not connected with revelant issues, and also with matters concerning the Goetheanum—you know that my first literary activity is associated with the name of Goethe and that it was developed in a domain in which today, even for those who refuse to open their eyes, who prefer to remain asleep, the powerful catastrophic happenings of our time are adumbrated. My view of Goethe from the standpoint of spiritual science, and equally what I said recently in relation to *The Philosophy of Freedom*, are of course a personal matter; on the other hand, however, this personal factor is intimately linked with the march of events in recent decades. The origin of my *Philosophy of Freedom* and of my Goethe publications is closely connected with the fact that, up to the end of the eighties I lived in Austria and then moved to Germany, first to Weimar and then to Berlin, a connection of course that is purely external. But when we reflect upon this external connection we are gradually led, in the light of the facts, if we apprehend the symptoms aright, to an understanding of the inner significance. From the historical sketches I have outlined you will have observed that I am obliged to apply to life what I call historical symptomatology, that I must comprehend history as well as individual human lives from out of their symptoms and manifestations because they are pointers to the real inner happenings. One must really have the will to look beyond external facts in order to arrive at their inner meaning.

Many people today would like to learn to develop supersensible vision, but clairvoyance is difficult to achieve and

## Lecture VII

the majority would prefer to spare themselves the effort. That is why it is often the case today that for those naturally endowed with clairvoyance there is a dichotomy between their external life and their clairvoyant faculty. Indeed, where this dichotomy exists supersensible vision is of little value and is seldom able to transcend personal factors. Our epoch is an age of transition. Every epoch, of course, is an age of transition. It is simply a question of realizing what is transmitted. Something of importance is transmitted, something that touches man in his inmost being and is of vital importance for his inner life. If we examine objectively what the so-called educated public has pursued the world over in recent decades, we are left with a sorry picture—the picture of a humanity that is fast asleep. This is not intended as a criticism, nor as an invitation to pessimism, but as a stimulus to awaken in man those forces which will enable him to attain, at least provisionally, his most important goal, namely, to develop insight, real insight into things. Our present age must shed certain illusions and see things as they really are.

Do not begin by asking: what must I do, what must others do? For the majority of people today such questions are inopportune. The important question is: *how* do I gain insight into the present situation? When one has adequate insight, one will follow the right course. That which must be developed will assuredly be developed when we have the right insight or understanding. But this entails a change of outlook. Above all men must clearly recognize that external events are in reality simply symptoms of an inner process of evolution occurring in the field of the supersensible, a process that embraces not only historical life, but also every individual, every one of us in the fullness of our being.

Let me quote the example of Robert Hamerling[1] by way of illustration. Today we are very proud that we can apply

*From Symptom to Reality in Modern History*

the law of causality in all kinds of fields; but this is a fatal illusion. Those who are familiar with Hamerling's life know how important for his whole inner development was the following circumstance. After acting for a short time as a 'supply' teacher in Graz (i.e. a kind of temporary post before one is appointed to a permanent position in a Gymnasium) he was transferred to Trieste. From there he was able to spend several holidays in Venice. When we recall the ten years which Hamerling spent on the Adriatic coast—he divided his time between teaching in Trieste and visiting Venice—we see how he was fired with ardent enthusiasm for all that the south could offer him, how he derived spiritual nourishment for his later poetry from his experiences there. The real Hamerling, the Hamerling we know, would have been a different person if he had not spent the ten years in question in Trieste with the opportunity for holidays in Venice!

Now supposing some thoroughly philistine professor is writing a biography of Hamerling and wanted to know how it was that Hamerling came to be transferred to Trieste precisely at this decisive moment in his life, and how a man without means, who was entirely dependent upon his salary, happened to be transferred to Trieste at this particular moment. I will give you the external explanation. Hamerling, as I have said, held at that time a temporary appointment (he was a supply teacher, as we say in Austria) at the Gymnasium[2] n Graz. These supply teachers are anxious to find a permanent appointment, and since this is a matter for the authorities, the applicant for such a post has to send in his various qualifications—written on one side of the application form—enclosing testimonials, etcetera. The application is then forwarded to a higher authority who in turn forwards it to still higher authorities, etcetera, etcetera. There is no need to describe the procedure further. The headmaster of

## Lecture VII

the Gymnasium in Graz where Hamerling worked as a temporary assistant, was the worthy Kaltenbrunner. Hamerling heard that there was a vacancy for a master in Budapest. At that time the Dual Monarchy did not exist and teachers could be transferred from Graz to Budapest and from Budapest to Graz. Hamerling applied for the post in Budapest and handed in his application, written in copper plate, together with the necessary testimonials to the headmaster, the worthy Kaltenbrunner, who placed it in a drawer and forgot all about it. Consequently the post in Budapest was given to another candidate. Hamerling was not appointed because Kaltenbrunner had forgotten to forward the application to the higher authorities, who, if they had not forgotten to do so, would have forwarded it to their immediate superiors and these in their turn to their superiors, etcetera, until it reached the minister, when it would have been referred back to the lower echelons and have passed down the bureaucratic ladder. Thus another candidate was appointed to the post in Budapest, and Hamerling spent the ten years which were decisive for his life, not in Budapest, but in Trieste, because sometime later a post fell vacant here to which he was appointed—and because, of course, the worthy Kaltenbrunner did not forget Hamerling's application a second time!

From the external point of view therefore Kaltenbrunner's negligence was responsible for the decisive turning point in Hamerling's life; otherwise Hamerling would have stagnated in Budapest. This is not intended as a cticicism of Budapest; but the fact remains that Budapest would have been a spiritual desert for Hamerling and he would have been unable to develop his particular talents. And our biographer would now be able to tell us how it was that Hamerling had been transferred from Graz to Trieste—

*From Symptom to Reality in Modern History*

because Kaltenbrunner had simply overlooked Hamerling's application.

Now this is a striking incident and one could find countless others of its kind in life. And he who seeks to measure life by the yard-stick of external events will scarcely find causes, even if he believes that he is able to establish causal relationships, that are more closely connected with their effects than the negligence of the worthy Kaltenbrunner with the spiritual development of Robert Hamerling. I make this observation simply to call your attention to the fact that it is imperative to implant in the hearts of men this principle: that external life as it unfolds must be seen simply as a symptom that reveals its inner meaning.

In my last lecture I spoke of the forties to the seventies as the critical period for the bourgeoisie. I pointed out how the bourgeoisie had been asleep during these critical years and how the end of the seventies saw the beginning of those fateful decades which led to our present situation.\* I spent the first years of these decades in Austria. Now as an Austrian living in the last third of the nineteenth century one was in a strange position if one wished to participate in the cultural life of the time. It is of course easy for me to throw light on this situation from the standpoint of a young man who spent his formative years in Austria and who was German by descent and racial affiliation. To be a German in Austria is totally different from being a German in the Reich† or in Switzerland. One must, of course, endeavour to understand everything in life and one can understand everything; one can adapt oneself to everything. But if, for example, one were to raise the question: what does an Austro-German feel about the social structure in which he lives and is it possible for an Austro-German without first having

\* I.e. the war of 1914–18.
† I.e. Imperial Germany.

## Lecture VII

adapted himself to it, to have any understanding of that peculiar civic consciousness one finds in Switzerland? Then the answer to this question must be an emphatic no! The Austro-German grew up in an environment that makes it totally impossible for him to understand—unless he forced himself to do so artificially—that inflexible civic consciousness peculiar to the Swiss.

But these national differentiations are seldom taken into account. We must however give heed to them if we are to understand the difficult problems in this domain which face us now and in the immediate future. It was significant that I spent my formative years in an environment where the most important things did not really concern me. I would not mention this if it were not in fact the most important experience of the true-born German-Austrian. In some it finds expression in one way, in others in another way. To some extent I lived as a typical Austrian. From the age of eleven to eighteen I had to cross twice a day the river Leitha which formed the frontier between Austria and Hungary since I lived at Neudörfl in Hungary and attended school in Wiener-Neustadt. It was an hour's journey on foot and a quarter of an hour's by slow train—there were no fast trains, nor are there any today I believe—and each time I had to cross the frontier. Thus one came to know the two faces of what is called abroad 'Austria'. Formerly things were not so easy in the Austrian half of the Empire. Today one cannot say things are easier (that is unlikely), but different. Up till now one had to distinguish two parts of the Austrian Empire. Officially one half was called, not Austria, but 'the Kingdoms and "lands" represented in the Federal Council', i.e. Cis-Leithania,[3] which included Galicia, Bohemia, Silesia, Moravia, Upper and Lower Austria, Salzburg, the Tyrol, Styria, Carniola, Carinthia, Istria and Dalmatia. The other half, Trans-Leithania,[3] consisted of the 'lands' of the Crown of St. Stephen, i.e. what is called abroad Hungary, which included also Croatia and Slavonia. Then, after the eighties, there was the territory of Bosnia and Herzegovina, occupied up to 1909 and later annexed, which was jointly administered by the two halves of the Empire.

Now in the area where I lived, even amongst the most important centres of interest, I did not find anything which really interested me between the ages of eleven and eighteen. The first important landmark was Frohsdorf, a castle inhabited by Count de Chambord, a member of the Bourbon family, who had made an unsuccessful attempt in 1871 to ascend the throne of France under the name of Henry V. There were many other peculiarities attaching to him. He was an ardent supporter of clericalism. In him, and in everything associated with him, one could perceive a world in decline, one could catch the atmosphere of a world that was crumbling in ruins. There were many things one saw there, but they were of no interest. And one felt: here is something which was once considered to be of the greatest importance and which many today still regard as immensely important. But in reality it is a bagatelle and has no particular importance.

The second thing in the neighbourhood was a Jesuit monastery, a genuine Jesuit monastery. The monks were called Redemptorists,[4] an offshoot of the Jesuits. This monastery was situated not far from Frohsdorf. One saw the monks perambulating, one learned of the aims and aspirations of the Jesuits, one heard various tales about them, but this too was of no interest. And again one felt: what has all this to do with the future evolution of mankind? One felt that these monks in their black cowls were totally unrelated to the real forces which are preparing man's future development.

## Lecture VII

The third thing in the locality where I lived was a masonic lodge. The local priest used to inveigh against it, but of course the lodge meant nothing to me for one was not permitted to enter. It is true the porter allowed me on one occasion to look inside, but in strict secrecy. On the following Sunday, however, I again heard the priest fulminating against the lodge. In brief, this too was something that did not concern me.

I was therefore well prepared when I matured and became more aware to be influenced by things which formerly held no interest for me. I regard it as very significant and a fortunate dispensation of my karma that, whilst I had been deeply interested in the spiritual world in my early years, in fact I lived my early life on the spiritual plane, I had not been forced by external circumstances into the classical education of the Gymnasium. All that one acquires through a humanistic education I acquired later on my own initiative. At that time the standard of the Gymnasium education in Austria was not too bad; it has progressively deteriorated since the seventies and of recent years has come perilously close to the educational system of neighbouring states. But looking back today I am glad that I was not sent to the Gymnasium in Wiener-Neustadt. I was sent to the Realschule[2] and thus came in touch with a teaching that prepared the ground for a modern way of thinking, a teaching that enabled me to be closely associated with a scientific outlook. I owed this association with scientific thinking to the fact that the best teachers—and they were few and far between—in the Austrian Realschule, which was organized on the most modern lines, were those who were connected in some way with modern scientific thinking.

This was not always true of the school in Wiener-Neustadt. In the lower classes—in the Austrian Realschule religious instruction was given only in the four lower classes—we had

## From Symptom to Reality in Modern History

a teacher of religion who was a very pleasant fellow, but was quite unfitted to bring us up as devout and pious Christians. He was a Catholic priest and that he was hardly fitted to inspire piety in us is shown by the fact that three young boys who used to call for him everyday after school were said to be his sons. But I still hold him in high regard for everything he taught in class apart from his religious instruction. He imparted this religious instruction in the following way: he called on a pupil to read a few pages from a devotional work; then it was set for homework. One did not understand a word, learned it by heart and received high marks, but of course one had not the slightest idea of the contents. His conversation outside the classroom was sometimes beautiful and stimulating and above all warm and friendly.

Now in such a school one passed through the hands of a succession of teachers of widely different calibre. All this is of symptomatic significance. We had two Carmelites as teachers, one was supposed to teach us French, the other English. The latter in particular scarcely knew a word of English; in fact he could not string together a complete sentence. In natural history we had a man who had not the faintest understanding of God and the world. But we had excellent teachers for mathematics, physics, chemistry and especially for projective geometry. And it was they who paved the way for this inner link with scientific thinking. It is to this scientific thinking that I owed the impulse which is fundamentally related to the future aims of mankind today.

When, after struggling through the Realschule one entered the University, one could not avoid—unless one was asleep—taking an interest in public affairs and the world around. Now the Austro-German—and this is important—arrives at a knowledge of the German make-up in a totally different way from the Reich German.[5] One could have, for example, a superficial interest in Austrian state-affairs, but one could

## Lecture VII

scarcely feel a real inner relationship to them if one were interested in the evolution of mankind. On the other hand, as in my own case, one could have recourse to the achievements of German culture at the end of the eighteenth and at the beginning of the nineteenth century and to what I should like to call Goetheanism. As an Austro-German one responds to this differently from the Reich German. One should not forget that once one has become inured to the natural scientific outlook through a modern education one outgrows a certain artificial milieu which has spread over the whole of Western Austria in recent time. One outgrows the clerical Catholicism to which the people of Western Austria only nominally adhere, an extremely pleasant people for the most part—I exclude myself of course. This clerical Catholicism has never touched their lives deeply.

In the form it has assumed in western Austria this clerical Catholicism is a product of the Counter-Reformation, of the 'Hausmacht' policy of the Hapsburgs. The ideas and impulses of Protestantism were fairly widespread in Austria, but the Thirty Years' War and the events connected with it enabled the Hapsburgs to initiate a counter Reformation and to impose upon the extremely gifted and intelligent Austro-German people that terrible obscurantism, which *must* be imposed when one diffuses Catholicism in the form which prevailed in Austria as a consequence of the Counter Reformation. Consequently men's relationship to religion and religious issues becomes extremely superficial. And happiest are those who are still aware of this superficial relationship. The others who believe that their faith, their piety is honest and sincere are unwittingly victims of a monstrous illusion, of a terrible lie which destroys the inner life of the soul.

With a background of natural science it is impossible of course to come to terms with this frightful psychic mishmash which invades the soul. But there are always a few isolated individuals who develop themselves and stand apart from it. They find themselves driven towards the cultural life which reached its zenith in Central Europe at the end of the eighteenth and in the early nineteenth century. They came in touch with the current of thought which began with Lessing, was carried forward by Herder, Goethe and the German Romantics and which in its wider context can be called Goetheanism.

In these decades it was of decisive importance for the Austro-German with spiritual aspirations that—living outside the folk community to which Lessing, Goethe, Herder etcetera belonged, and transplanted into a wholly alien environment over the frontier—he imbibed there the spiritual perception of Goethe, Schiller, Lessing and Herder. Nothing else impressed one; one imbibed only the *Weltanschauung* of Weimar classicism—and in this respect one stood apart, isolated and alone. For again one was surrounded by those phenomena which did not concern one.

And so one was associated with something that one gradually felt to be second nature, something, however, that was uprooted from its native soil and which one cherished in one's inmost soul in a community which was interested only in superficialities. For it was anomalous to cherish Goethean ideas at a time when the world around was enthusiastic—but the words of enthusiasm were pompous and artificial, without any suggestion of sincere and honest endeavour—about such publications (and I could give other examples) as the book of the then Crown Prince Rudolf *An illustrated history of Austria*. The book in fact was the work of ghost writers. One had no affinity with this trash, though, it is true, one belonged outwardly to this world of superficiality. One treasured in one's soul that which was an expression of the Central European spirit and which in a wider context I should like to call Goetheanism.

## Lecture VII

This Goetheanism, with which I associate the names of Schiller, Lessing, Herder and also the German philosophers, occupies a singularly isolated position in the world. And this isolation is extremely significant for the whole evolution of modern mankind for it causes those who wish to embark upon a serious study of Goetheanism to become a little reflective.

Looking back over the past one asks oneself: what have Lessing, Goethe and the later German Romantics, approximately up to the middle of the nineteenth century, contributed to the world? In what respect is this contribution related to the historical evolution prior to Lessing's time? Now it is well known that the emergence of Protestantism out of Catholicism is intimately connected with the historical evolution of Central Europe. We see, on the one hand, in Central Europe, in Germany for example—I have already discussed the same phenomenon in relation to Austria—the survival of the universalist impulse of Roman Catholicism. In Austria its influence was more external, as I have described, in Germany more inward. Now there is a vast difference between the Austrian Catholic and the Bavarian Catholic, and many of these differences which have survived date back to the remote past. Then came the invasion of Catholic culture by Protestantism or Lutheranism, which in Switzerland took the form of Calvinism or Zwinglianism.[6] Now a high proportion of the German people, especially the Reich Germans, was Lutheran. But strangely enough there is no connection whatsoever between Lutheranism and Goetheanism! It is true that Goethe had studied both Lutheranism and Catholicism, though somewhat superficially. But when one considers the ferment in Goethe's soul, one can only say that throughout his life it was a matter of indifference to him whether one professed Catholicism or Protestantism. Both confessions could be found in his entourage, but he was in no way connected with them. To this aperçu the following can be added. Herder[7] was pastor and later General Superintendent in Weimar. As pastor, of course, he had received much from Luther externally and was familiar with his teachings; he was aware that his outlook and thinking had nothing in common with Lutheranism and that he had entirely outgrown the Lutheran faith. Thus, in everything associated with Goetheanism—and I include men such as Herder and others—we have in this respect a completely isolated phenomenon. When we enquire into the nature of this isolated phenomenon we find that Goetheanism is a crystallization of all kinds of impulses of the fifth post-Atlantean epoch. Luther did not have the slightest influence on Goethe; Goethe, however, was influenced by Linnaeus,[8] Spinoza and Shakespeare, and on his own admission these three personalities exercised the greatest influence upon his spiritual development.

Thus Goetheanism stands out as an isolated phenomenon and that is why it can never become popular. For the old entrenched positions persist; not even the slightest attempt was made to promote the ideas of Lessing, Schiller, and Goethe amongst the broad masses of the population, let alone to encourage the feelings and sentiments of these personalities. Meanwhile an outmoded Catholicism on the one hand, and an outmoded Lutheranism on the other hand, lived on as relics from the past. And it is a significant phenomenon that, within the cultural stream to which Goethe belonged and which produced a Goethe, the spiritual activities of the people are influenced by the sermons preached by the Protestant pastors. Amongst the latter are a few who are receptive to modern culture, but that is of no help to them in their sermons. The spiritual nourishment offered by the church today is antediluvian and is totally unrelated to the demands of the time; it cannot lend in any

## Lecture VII

way vitality or vigour. It is associated, however, with another aspect of our culture, that aspect which is responsible for the fact that the spiritual life of the majority of mankind is divorced from reality. Perhaps the most significant symptom of modern bourgeois philistinism is that its spiritual life is remote from reality, all its talk is empty and unreal.

Such phenomena, however, are usually ignored, but as symptoms they are deeply significant. You can read the literature of the war-mongers over recent decades and you will find that Kant is quoted again and again. In recent weeks many of these war-mongers have turned pacifist, since peace is now in the offing. But that is of no consequence; philistines they still remain, that is the point. The Stresemann[9] of today is the same Stresemann of six weeks ago. And today it is customary to quote Kant as the ideal of the pacifists. This is quite unreal. These people have no understanding of the source from which they claim to have derived their spiritual nourishment.

That is one of the most characteristic features of the present time and accounts for the strange fact that a powerful spiritual impulse, that of Goetheanism, has met with total incomprehension. In face of the present catastrophic events this thought fills us with dismay. When we ask: what will become of this wave—one of the most important in the fifth post-Atlantean epoch—given the atmosphere prevailing in the world today, we are filled with sadness.

In the light of this situation the decision to call the centre which wishes to devote its activities to the most important impulses of the fifth post-Atlantean epoch the 'Goetheanum' irrespective of the fate which may befall it, has a certain importance. That this building shall bear the name 'Goetheanum' for many years to come is of no consequence; what is important is that the thought even existed, the thought of using the name 'Goetheanum' in these most difficult times.

*From Symptom to Reality in Modern History*

Precisely through the fact I have mentioned to you, Goetheanism in its isolation could become something of unique importance when one lived at the aforesaid time in Austria where one's interests were limited. For if people had understood that Goetheanism was something which concerned them, the present catastrophe would not have arisen. This and many other factors enabled isolated individuals in the German-speaking areas of Austria—the broad masses live under the heel of the Catholicism of the Counter-Reformation—to develop a deep inner relationship to Goetheanism. I made the acquaintance of one of these personalities, Karl Julius Schröer[10] who lived and worked in Austria. In every field in which he worked he was inspired by the Goethe impulse. History will one day record what men such as Karl Julius Schröer thought about the political needs of Austria in the second half of the nineteenth century. These people who never found a hearing were aware to some extent how the present situation could have been avoided, but that it was nevertheless inevitable because no one would listen to them.

On arriving in Imperial Germany one had above all the impression, when one had developed a close spiritual affinity with Goethe, that there was nowhere any understanding of this affinity. I came to Weimar in autumn 1889—I have already described the pleasing aspects of life in Weimar—but what I treasured in Goethe (I had already published my first important book on Goethe) met with little understanding or sympathy because it was the spiritual element in him that I valued. Outwardly and inwardly life in Weimar was wholly divorced from any connection with Goethean impulses. In fact these Goethean impulses were completely unknown in the widest circles, especially amongst professors of the history of literature who lectured on Goethe, Lessing and Herder in the universities—unknown amongst

## Lecture VII

the philistines who perpetrated the most atrocious biographies of Goethe. I could only find consolation for these horrors by reading the publications of Schröer and the excellent book of Herman Grimm which I came across relatively early in my life. But Herman Grimm was never taken seriously by the universities. They regarded him as a dilettante, not as a serious scholar.

No genuine university scholar of course has ever made the effort to take K. J. Schröer seriously; he is always treated as a light-weight. I could give many examples of this. But one should not forget that the literary world with its many ramifications—including, if I may say so, journalism—has been under the influence of a bourgeoisie that has been declining in recent decades, a bourgeoisie which is fast asleep and which, when it embarks upon spiritual activities, has no understanding of their real meaning. Under these circumstances it is impossible of course to arrive at any understanding of Goetheanism. For Goethe himself is, in the best sense of the word, the most modern spirit of the fifth post-Atlantean epoch.

Consider for a moment his unique characteristics. First, his whole *Weltanschauung*—which can be raised to a higher spiritual level than Goethe himself could achieve—rests upon a solid scientific foundation. At the present time a firmly established *Weltanschauung* cannot exist without a scientific basis. That is why there is a strong scientific substratum to the book with which I concluded my Goethe studies in 1897. (The book has now been republished for reasons similar to those which led to the re-issue of *The Philosophy of Freedom*.) The solid body of philistines said at that time (it was a time when my books were still reviewed—the title of the book is *Goethe's Conception of the World*[*]):

[*] Anthroposophical Publishing Co., London and Anthroposophic Press, New York, 1928.

in reality he ought to call it 'Goethe's conception of nature'. The so-called Goethe scholars, the literary historians, philosophers and the like failed to realize that it is impossible to present Goethe's *Weltanschauung* unless it is firmly anchored in his conception of nature.

A second characteristic which shows Goethe to be the most modern spirit of the fifth post-Atlantean age is the way in which that peculiar spiritual path unfolds within him which leads from the intuitive perception of nature to art. In studying Goethe it is most interesting to follow this connection between perception of nature and artistic activity, between artistic creation and artistic imagination. One touches upon thousands of questions—which are not dry, theoretical questions, but questions instinct with life, when one studies this strange and peculiar process which always takes place in Goethe when he observes nature as an artist, but sees it on that account no less in its reality, and when he works as an artist in such a way that, to quote his own words, one feels art to be something akin to the continuation of divine creation in nature at a higher level.

A third characteristic typical of Goethe's *Weltanschauung* is his conception of man. He sees him as an integral part of the universe, as the crowning achievement of the entire universe. Goethe always strives to see him, not as an isolated being, but imbued with the wisdom that informs nature. For Goethe the soul of man is the stage on which the spirit of nature contemplates itself. But these thoughts which are expressed here in abstract form have countless implications if they are pursued concretely. And all this constitutes the solid base on which we can build that which leads to the supreme heights of spiritual supersensible perception in the present age. If one points out today that mankind as a whole has failed to give serious attention to Goethe—and it has failed in this respect—has failed to develop any relation-

## Lecture VII

ship to Goetheanism, then it is certainly not in order to criticize, lecture or reproach mankind as a whole, but simply to invite them to undertake a serious study of Goetheanism. For to pursue the path of Goetheanism is to open the doors to an anthroposophically orientated spiritual science. And without Anthroposophy the world will not find a way out of the present catastrophic situation. In many ways the safest approach to spiritual science is to begin with the study of Goethe.

All this is related to something else. I have already pointed out that this shallow spiritual life which is preached from the pulpit and which then becomes for many a living lie of which they are unconscious—all this is outmoded. And fundamentally the erudition in all the faculties of our universities is equally outmoded. This erudition becomes an anomaly where Goetheanism exists alongside it. For a further characteristic feature of Goethe's personality is his phenomenal universality. It is true that in various domains Goethe has sowed only the first seeds, but these seeds can be cultivated everywhere and when cultivated contain the germ of something great and grandiose, the great modern impulse which mankind prefers to ignore, and compared with which modern university education in its outlook and attitude is antediluvian. Even though it accepts new discoveries, this modern university education is out of date. But at the same time there exists a true life of the spirit, Goetheanism, which is ignored. In a certain sense Goethe is the *universitas litterarum*, the hidden university, and in the sphere of the spiritual life it is the university education of today that usurps the throne. Everything that takes place in the external world and which has led to the present catastophe is, in the final analysis, the result of what is taught in our universities. People talk today of this or that in politics, of certain personalities, of the rise of socialism, of the good and bad aspects of art, of Bolshevism, etcetera; they are afraid of what may happen in the future, they envisage such and such occupying a certain post, and there are those who six weeks ago said the opposite of what they say today ... such is the state of affairs. Where does all this originate? Ultimately in the educational institutions of the present day. Everything else is of secondary importance if people fail to see that the axe must be laid to the tree of modern education. What is the use of developing endless so-called clever ideas, if people do not realize where in fact the break with the past must be made.

I have already spoken of certain things which did not concern me. I can now tell you of something else which did not concern me. When I left the Realschule for the university I entered my name for different lecture courses and attended various lectures. But they held no interest for me; one felt that they were quite out of touch with the impulse of our time. Without wishing to appear conceited I must confess that I had a certain sympathy for that *universitas*, Goetheanism, because Goethe also found that his university education held little interest for him. And at the royal university of Leipzig in the (then) Kingdom of Saxony, and again at Strasbourg university in later years, he took virtually no interest in the lectures he attended. And yet everything, even the quintessence of the artistic in Goethe rests upon the solid foundation of a rigorous observation of nature. In spite of all university education he gradually became familiar with the most modern impulses, even in the sphere of knowledge. When we speak of Goetheanism we must not lose sight of this. And this is what I should have liked to bring to men's attention in my Goethe studies and in my book *Goethe's Conception of the World*. I should have liked to make them aware of the real Goethe. But the time for this was not ripe; to a large extent the response was lacking. As I men-

## Lecture VII

tioned recently the first indications were visible in Weimar where the soil was to some extent favourable. But nothing fruitful came of it. Those who were already in entrenched positions barred the way to those who could have brought a new creative impulse. If the modern age were imbued in some small measure with Goetheanism, it would long for spiritual science, for Goetheanism prepares the ground for the reception of spiritual science. Then Goetheanism would again become a means whereby a real regeneration of mankind today could be achieved. One cannot afford to take a superficial view of our present age.

After my lecture in Basel yesterday* I felt that no honest scientist could deny what I had to say on the subject of supersensible knowledge if he were prepared to face the facts. There are no logical grounds for rejecting spiritual knowledge; the real cause for rejection is to be found in that barbarism which in all regions of the civilized world is responsible for the present catastrophe. It is profoundly symbolic that a few years ago a Goethe society had nothing better to do than to appoint as president a former finance minister—a typical example of men's remoteness from what they profess to honour. This finance minister who, as I said recently, bears, perhaps symptomatically, the Christian name 'Kreuzwendedich' believes of course, in his fond delusion, that he pays homage to Goethe. With a background of modern education he has no idea and can have no idea how far, how infinitely far removed he is from the most elementary understanding of Goetheanism.

The climate of the present epoch is unsuited to a deeper understanding of Goetheanism. For Goetheanism has no national affiliation, it is not something specifically German. It draws nourishment from Spinoza, from Shakespeare,

* *Rechtfertigung der übersinnlichen Erkenntnis durch die Naturwissenschaft*, 31st October, 1918 (see Bibl. Nr. 72).

from Linnaeus—none of whom is of German origin. Goethe himself admitted that these three personalities exercised a profound influence upon him—and in this he was not mistaken. (He who knows Goethe recognizes how justified this admission is.) Goetheanism could determine men's thinking, their religious life, every branch of science, the social forms of community life, the political life . . . it could reign supreme everywhere. But the world today listens to windbags such as Eucken[11] or Bergson[11] and the like . . . (I say nothing of the political babblers, for in this realm today adjective and substantive are almost identical).

What we have striven for here—and which will arouse such intense hatred in the future that its realization is problematical, especially at the present time—is a living protest against the alienation of spiritual life today from reality. And this protest is best expressed by saying: what we wanted to realize here is a Goetheanum. When we speak here of a Goetheanum we bear witness to the most important characteristics and also to the most important demands of our time. And amid the philistine world of today this Goetheanum at least has been *willed* and should tower above this present world that claims to be civilized.

Of course, if the wishes of many contemporaries had been fulfilled, one could perhaps say that it would have been more sensible to speak of a Wilsonianum,[12] for that is the flag under which the present epoch sails. And it is to Wilsonism that the world at the present time is prepared to submit and probaly will submit.

Now it may seem strange to say that the sole remedy against Wilsonism is Goetheanism. Those who claim to know better come along and say: the man who talks like this is a utopian, a visionary. But who are these people who coin this phrase: he is an innocent abroad—who are they? Why, none other than those worldly men who are respons-

## Lecture VII

ible for the present state of affairs, who always imagined themselves to be essentially 'practical' men. It is they of course who refuse to listen to words of profound truth, namely, that Wilsonism will bring sickness upon the world, and in all domains of life the world will be in need of a remedy and this remedy will be Goetheanism.

Permit me to conclude with a personal observation on the interpretation of my book *Goethe's Conception of the World* which has now appeared in a second edition. Through a strange concatenation of circumstances the book has not yet arrived; one is always ready to make allowances, especially at the present time. It was suggested by men of 'practical' experience some time ago, months ago in fact, that my books *The Philosophy of Freedom* and *Goethe's Conception of the World* should be forwarded here direct from the printers and so avoid going via Berlin and arrive here more quickly. One would have thought that those who proffered this advice were knowledgeable in these matters. I was informed that *The Philosophy of Freedom* had been despatched, but after weeks and weeks had not arrived. For some time people had been able to purchase copies in Berlin. None was to be had here because somewhere on the way the matter had been in the hands of the 'practical' people and we unpractical people were not supposed to interfere. What had happened? The parcel had been handed in by the 'practical' people of the firm who had been told to send it to Dornach near Basel. But the gentleman responsible for the despatch said to himself: Dornach near Basel; that is in Alsace, for there is a Dornach there which is also near Basel . . . there is no need to pay foreign postage, German stamps will suffice. And so, on 'practical' instructions the parcel went to Dornach in Alsace where, of course, they had no idea what to do with it. The matter had to be taken up by the unpractical people here. Finally, after long delays when the 'practical' gentleman had satisfied himself that Dornach near Basel is not Dornach in Alsace, *The Philosophy of Freedom* arrived. Whether the other book, *Goethe's Conception of the World*, instead of being sent from Stuttgart to Dornach near Basel has been sent by some 'practical' person via the North Pole, to arrive finally in Dornach after travelling round the globe, I cannot say. In any case, this is only one example that we have experienced personally of the 'practical' man's contribution to the practical affairs of daily life.

This is what I was first able to undertake personally in a realm that lay close to my heart—more through external circumstances than through my own inclination—in order to be of service to the epoch. And when I consider what was the purpose of my various books, which are born of the impulse of the time, I believe that these books answer the demands of our epoch in widely divergent fields. They have taught me how powerful have been the forces in recent decades acting against the spirit of the age. However much in their ruthlessness people may believe that they can achieve their aims by force, the fact remains that nothing in reality can be enforced which runs counter to the impulses of the time. Many things which are in keeping with the impulses of the time can be delayed; but if they are delayed they will later find scope for expression, perhaps under another name and in a totally different context. I believe that these two books, amongst other things, can show how, by observing one's age, one can be of service to it. One can serve one's age in every way, in the simplest and most humble activities. One must simply have the courage to take up Goetheanism which exists as a *Universitas liberarum scientiarum* alongside the antediluvian university that everyone admires today, the socialists of the extreme left most of all.

It might easily appear as if these remarks are motivated

## Lecture VII

by personal animosity and therefore I always hesitate to express them. One is of course a target for the obvious accusation—'Aha, this fellow abuses universities because he failed to become a university professor!' ... One must put up with this facile criticism when it is necessary to show that those who advocate this or that from a political, scientific, political-economic or confessional point of view of some kind or other fail to put their finger on the real malady of our time. Only those point to the real malady who draw attention to the pernicious dogma of infallibility which, through the fatal concurrence of mankind has led to the surrender of everything to the present domination of science, to those centres of official science where the weeds grow abundantly, alongside a few healthy plants of course. I am not referring to a particular individual or particular university professor (any more than when I speak of states or nations I am referring to a particular state or nation)—they may be excellent people, that is not the point. The really important question is the *nature of the system*.

And how serious this situation is, is shown by the fact that the technical colleges which have begun to lose a little of their natural character now assume university airs and so have gone rapidly downhill and become corrupted by idleness.

I want you to consider the criticisms I have made today as a kind of interlude in our anthroposophical discussions. But I think that the present epoch offers such a powerful challenge to our thoughts and sentiments in this direction that these enquiries must be undertaken by us especially because, unfortunately, they will not be undertaken elsewhere.

Our present age is still very far removed from Goetheanism, which certainly does not imply studying the life and works of Goethe alone. Our epoch sorely needs to turn to

## From Symptom to Reality in Modern History

Goetheanism in all spheres of life. This may sound utopian and impractical, but it is the most practical answer at the present time. When the different spheres of life are founded on Goetheanism we shall achieve something totally different from the single achievement of the bourgeoisie today—rationalism. He who is grounded in Goetheanism will assuredly find his way to spiritual science. This is what one would like to inscribe in letters of fire in the souls of men today.

This has been my aim for decades. But much of what I have said from the depths of my heart and which was intended to be of service to the age has been received by my contemporaries as an edifying Sunday afternoon sermon—for in reality those who are happy in their cultural sleep ask nothing more. We must seek concretely to discover what the epoch demands, what is necessary for our age—this is what mankind so urgently needs today. And above all we must endeavour to gain insight into this, for today insight is all important. Amidst the vast confusion of our time, a confusion that will soon become worse confounded, it is futile to ask: what must the individual do? What he must do first and foremost is to strive for insight and understanding so that the infallibility in the domain that I referred to today is directed into the right channel.

My book *Goethe's Conception of the World* was written specially in order to show that in the sphere of knowledge there are two streams today: a decadent stream which everyone admires, and another stream which contains the most fertile seeds for the future, and which everyone avoids. In recent decades men have suffered many painful experiences—and often through their own fault. But they should realize that they have suffered most—and worse is still to follow—at the hands of their schoolmasters of whom they are so proud. It appears that mankind must needs pass

## *Lecture VII*

through the experiences which they have to undergo at the hands of the world schoolmaster, for they have contrived in the end to set up a schoolmaster as world organizer. Those windbags who have persuaded the world with their academic twaddle are now joined by another who proposes to set the world to right with empty academic rhetoric.

I have no wish to be pessimistic. These words are spoken in order to awaken those impulses which will answer Wilsonism with Goetheanism. They are not inspired by any kind of national sentiment, for Goethe himself was certainly not a nationalist; his genius was universal. The world must be preserved from the havoc that would follow if Wilsonism were to replace Goetheanism!

## LECTURE VIII

We have attempted so far to throw light from many different points of view upon the characteristic features of the fifth post-Atlantean epoch in which we are now living and which began in the early fifteenth century (1413) and will end in the middle of the fourth millennium. Now many of the symptomatic events of today are closely associated with the events which occurred at the beginning of this epoch. For reasons which will become evident in the course of the following lectures and which are connected with the whole of human evolution, the fifth post-Atlantean epoch can be subdivided into five stages. We have now reached a moment of particular importance, the decisive turning point when the first fifth of this epoch passes over into the second fifth.

I propose to give you a general survey of the impulses which have determined the history of religions, in so far as they are symptomatic of this fifth post-Atlantean epoch. Many things which I shall say in the course of this survey cannot be more than pointers or indications. For when we embark upon a serious study of the religious impulses of mankind the facts we have to consider are so difficult to convey owing to the limitations of language that we can only discuss them approximately; we can only hint at them. And you must therefore endeavour to read between the lines of what I shall say today and tomorrow, not because I wish to be a mystery monger, but because language is too powerless to express adequately the multiplicity and variety of impulses of spiritual reality. Above all I must call your attention today to the fact that he who studies these things

## Lecture VIII

from the standpoint of spiritual science must really be prepared to think and reflect. Today mankind has more or less lost the habit of thinking. I do not mean, of course, the thinking that is the proud boast of modern science, but the thinking which is capable of distinguishing precisely between different forms of reality. In order to be able to study what we are now called upon to examine, I must remind you that I have already spoken of the two currents in the evolution of mankind. I do not know whether all those present here listened so carefully to the expressions I coined in the course of my previous lectures that they have already noticed what I wish to underline especially today, so that no misunderstanding shall arise in the following observations.

In the evolution of post-Atlantean humanity I emphasized one thing in particular, namely that mankind of the post-Atlantean epoch matures progressively at an ever earlier age. In the first post-Atlantean epoch, that of ancient India, men remained capable of developing physically up to the age of fifty; in the ancient Persian epoch development ceased at an earlier age, and in the Egypto-Chaldaean epoch at an even earlier age. In the Graeco-Latin epoch development was only possible up to the age of thirty-five and in our present epoch, as a consequence of natural development, men cease to develop beyond the age of twenty-eight. Any further development must be derived from spiritual impulses. Then, in the sixth post-Atlantean epoch, mankind will be unable to develop after the age of twenty-one—and so on. With the passage of time, therefore, mankind matures physically at an ever earlier age.

It is important to bear in mind that this evolution I have just mentioned involves the whole of mankind. In relation to this first current of evolution, as I shall call it, we can say that mankind is at the stage of development which the individual experiences between the ages of twenty-eight and twenty-one. These are the years when the Sentient Soul especially is developed. We are therefore at a stage in evolution when mankind as a whole is in process of developing especially the Sentient Soul. Such is the one current of evolution.

Now I have already spoken of another current of evolution. In this second evolution, in the first post-Atlantean epoch, that of ancient India, the individual developed his etheric body; in the second post-Atlantean epoch, that of ancient Persia, he developed the sentient body; in the Egypto-Chaldaean epoch the sentient soul, in the Graeco-Latin epoch the intellectual or mind soul, and in the present epoch the consciousness soul. Such is the second current of evolution. The first current of evolution which concerns the whole of mankind runs its course concurrently with the second evolution which concerns the isolated individual within the body of mankind. To repeat, the isolated individual develops the Consciousness Soul in the present epoch.

The third current of evolution to be considered is that which shows the development of the different peoples over the whole earth. In this context I have already pointed out that the Italian people, for example, develops in particular the Sentient Soul, the French people the Intellectual or Mind Soul and the English speaking peoples the Consciousness Soul. This is the third current of evolution. These currents are loosely intermingled and I am unable to point to any particular principle that is characteristic of our present epoch.

*First Evolution*     *Second Evolution*
The whole of mankind develops the Sentient Soul.     The individual develops the Consciousness Soul.
*Third Evolution*
The evolution of the different peoples.

## Lecture VIII

These three currents of evolution meet and cross in every human being; they invade every individual soul. The world order is by no means simple! If, for your benefit, you want the world order to be explained in the simplest terms, then you must become either professor or King of Spain. You will recall the legend of the King of Spain who declared, when a much less complicated cosmic system than the one envisaged here was explained to him: had God entrusted the ordering of the world to him he would not have made it so complicated, he would have simplified things. And certain text-books or other popular encyclopaedias have always followed the principle that truth of necessity must be simple! This principle is not adopted of course on rational grounds, but solely for reasons of convenience, I might even say, out of general human indolence. By systematic arrangement where everything is classified or catalogued one comes no nearer to reality. And those facile, I might even say, slick concepts much favoured today in the domain of the official sciences are light-years away from true reality.

If we wish to understand all that plays into the souls of men of this fifth post-Atlantean epoch we must bear in mind the part-evolution that intervenes in the total evolution of mankind. For this part-evolution proceeds slowly and gradually. In order to examine briefly the religious development of this epoch it will be necessary to keep this threefold evolution to some extent in the background. About the time when the fifth post-Atlantean epoch began, not only many things, but also the religious life of mankind was caught up in a movement that has repercussions, a movement that is by no means concluded today. We must have a profound understanding of this movement if men really wish to make use of the Consciousness Soul. For only when men arrive at a clear insight and understanding of what is happening in evolution will they be able to participate in the further development of mankind on earth.

Towards the beginning of the fifteenth century the first stirrings of the religious impulses are perceptible. Let us first look at these religious impulses in Europe for having seen them at work in Europe we shall also have a picture of their impact upon the rest of the world. The first religious stirrings had long been prepared—since the tenth century or even the ninth century in the spiritual life of Europe and the near East. And this was due to the fact that the after effect of the Christ impulse manifested itself in the civilized world in a very special way. This Christ impulse, as we know, is a continuous process. But this abstract statement—that the Christ impulse is a continuous process—says in reality very little. We must also ascertain in what way it acquires a distinct and separate character, in what way, in its differentiations, it is then modified, or better still, in what way it is metamorphosed and assumes widely different forms.

That which began to awaken at the beginning of the fifteenth century and which still exercises a profound influence on men today—often unconsciously and without their suspecting it—is related to the catastrophic events of the present time. And this is explained by the fact that from the ninth and tenth centuries onwards it was possible for the 'People of the Christ' to emerge in a certain territory within the civilized world, a people that was endowed with the special inborn capacity to become the vehicle of the Christ revelation for future generations. We express a profound truth when we say that in this epoch and in readiness for later times a people had been specially prepared by world events to become the People of the Christ.

This situation arose because, in the ninth century, that which continued to operate as the Christ impulse acquired, to some extent, a separate character in Europe and this

## Lecture VIII

differentiation is seen in the fact that certain souls showed themselves capable of receiving directly the revelation of the Christ impulse (i.e. this particular form of the Christ impulse), and that these souls were diverted towards Eastern Europe. And the consequence of the controversy between the Patriarch Photius[1] and Pope Nicholas I was that the Christ impulse in its particular intensity was diverted to the East of Europe.

As you know this led to the famous *filioque* controversy—the question whether the Holy Ghost proceeds from the Father and the Son, or from the Father only. But I do not wish to enter into disputes over dogma. I want to discuss that which has a lasting influence—that differentiation, that metamorphosis of the Christ impulse which is characterized by the fact that the inhabitants of Eastern Europe were receptive to the continual influx of the Christ impulse, to the continuous presence of the 'breath' of Christ. This particular form (or metamorphosis) of the Christ impulse was diverted to the East and in consequence, the Russian people, in the widest sense of the term, became, within the framework of European civilization, the People of the Christ.

It is particularly important to know this at the present time. Do not say in face of present events* that such a truth seems strange, for that would be to misunderstand the fundamental principle of spiritual wisdom, namely, that, paradoxically, external events often contradict their inner truth. That this contradiction may occur here and there is not important; what is important is that we recognize which are the inner processes, the true spiritual realities. For example, we have here the map of Europe (points to a diagram on the blackboard); we see sweeping eastwards since the ninth century that spiritual wave which led to the birth of the People of the Christ.

* I.e. the Russian Revolution.

*From Symptom to Reality in Modern History*

What do we mean by saying that the People of the Christ arose in the East? We mean by this—and it can be verified by studying the symptoms in external history; you will find, if you bear in mind the inner processes and not the external facts which often contradict reality that this statement is fully confirmed—we mean by this that a territory has been set apart in the East of Europe where lived men who were directly united with the Christ impulse. The Christ is ever present as an inner aura impregnating the thinking and feeling of this people.

One cannot find perhaps any clearer or more direct proof for what I have said here than the personality of Solovieff, the most outstanding Russian philosopher of modern times. Read him and you will feel—despite the peculiar characteristics of Solovieff which I have already discussed from other points of view—you will feel how there streams into him directly what could be called the Christ inspiration. This inspiration acts so powerfully within him that he cannot imagine the entire structure of social life otherwise than ordained by Christ the King, the Invisible Christ as sovereign of the social community. To Solovieff everything is imbued with the Christ, every single action performed by man is permeated with the Christ impulse which penetrates even into the muscular system. The philosopher Solovieff is the purest and finest representative of the People of the Christ.

Here is the source of the entire Russian evolution up to the present day. And when we know that the Russian people is the People of the Christ we shall also be able to understand, as we shall see later, the present evolution in its present form. That is the one metamorphosis prepared by the People of the Christ one example of the differentiations of the Christ impulse.

The second differentiation of the Christ impulse was the work of Rome which, having diverted the authentic and

## Lecture VIII

continuous metamorphosis of the Christ impulse towards the East, transformed the spiritual sovereignty of Christ into the temporal sovereignty of the Church and decreed that everything relating to Christ had been revealed once and for all at the beginning of our era, that it had been a unique revelation never to be repeated. And this revelation had been entrusted to the Church and the task of the church was to bear witness to this revelation before the world. As a consequence, the Christian revelation became at the same time a question of temporal power and was taken over by the ecclesiastical authorities. It is important to bear this in mind because it meant no less than that the Christ impulse was thereby in part emasculated. The Christ impulse in its totality resides in the People of the Christ who transmit it in such a way that the Christ impulse actually continues to exercise a direct influence at the present time. The Church of Rome has interrupted this continuity, it has concentrated the Christ impulse upon a historical event at the beginning of our era and has attributed everything of a later date to tradition or written records, so that henceforth everything will be administered by the Church.

Thus, amongst the peoples over whom the Church of Rome extended its influence, the Christ impulse was dragged down from the spiritual heights (in the East it had always remained at this level) and was put at the service of political intrigue and was caught up in that tangled relationship between politics and the Church which, as I have already described to you from other points of view, was characteristic of the Middle Ages. In Russia, although the Czar had been nominated 'father' of the Russian Orthodox Church, this troubled alliance between politics and the Church did not really exist, it was only apparent in external events. An important secret of European evolution is here concealed. The real confusion of questions of power and problems of ecclesiastical administration originated in Rome.

This confusion of power politics and ecclesiastical administration, by reason of inner grounds of historical evolution, had reached a critical stage for the Christ impulse towards the beginning of the fifth post-Atlantean epoch. As you already know this epoch is the epoch of the Consciousness Soul when the personality asserts itself and seeks to become self-reliant. Consequently it is particularly difficult, after the birth of the autonomous personality, to come to terms with the question of the personality of Christ Jesus himself. Throughout the Middle Ages and up to the fifteenth century the Church had maintained its dogmas concerning the union of the divine and spiritual with the human and physical in the person of Christ. These dogmas of course had assumed different forms without provoking hitherto deep-seated spiritual conflicts. In those countries where Roman Catholicism had spread, these conflicts arose at a time when the personality, seeking to arrive at inner understanding of itself, also sought enlightenment upon the personality of Christ Jesus. In reality the controversies of Hus, Wyclif, Luther, Zwingli, Calvin, of the Anabaptists Kaspar Schwenkfeld, Sebastian Frank and others revolved round this question. They wanted clarification upon the relationship between the divine and spiritual nature of Christ and the human and physical nature of Jesus. This was the central question and of course it created a great stir. It raised many doubts about that current of evolution which had blunted the unbroken influence of the Christ impulse to such an extent that the Christ impulse was limited to a single event at the beginning of our era and was to be transmitted henceforth only by the Church authorities. And so we can say: all those who came under the influence of Rome became the 'People of the Church'. Churches and sects, etcetera, were founded which had a certain importance.

## Lecture VIII

But sects were also founded in Russia you will reply. Now to employ the same word which has different connotations in different areas is to lose all sense of reality. A study of Russian sects shows that they do not bear the slightest resemblance to the religious sects in the territories which at one time had been under the influence of the Church of Rome. It is not a question of designating things by the same term; what matters is the reality pulsating through them.

For reasons I have already mentioned, the life and aspirations of men at the beginning of the fifteenth century are characterized by a spirit of opposition to the uniformity of the Roman Church which operated through suggestionism.

This assault of personality again provokes a reaction— the counter-thrust of Jesuitism which comes to the support of the Romanism of the Church. Jesuitism in its original sense (though everything today, if you will forgive the brutal expression, is reduced to idle gossip and Jesuitism is on everyone's lips) is only possible within the Roman Catholic Church. For fundamentally Jesuitism is based on the following: whilst in the true People of the Christ the revelation of the Christ impulse remains in the supersensible world and does not descend into the physical world (Solovieff wishes to spiritualize the material world, not to materialize the spiritual world), the aim of Jesuitism is to drag down the Kingdom of God into the temporal world and to awaken impulses in the souls of men so that the Kingdom of God operates on the physical plane in the same way as the laws of the physical world. Jesuitism, therefore, aspires to establish a temporal sovereignty in the form of a temporal kingdom of the Christ. It wishes to achieve this by training the members of the Jesuit order after the fashion of an army. The individual Jesuit feels himself to be a spiritual soldier. He feels Christ, not as the spiritual Christ who acts upon the world through the medium of the Spirit, but he feels Him—and to this end he must direct his thoughts and feelings—as a temporal sovereign whom he serves as one serves an earthly King, or as a soldier serves his generalissimo. The ecclesiastical administration, since it is concerned with spiritual matters, will, of course, be different from that of a secular military regime; but the spiritual order must be subject to strict military discipline. Everything must be so ordained that the true Christian becomes a soldier of the generalissimo Jesus. In essence this is the purpose of those exercises which every Jesuit practises in order to develop in himself that vast power which the Jesuit order has long possessed and which will still be felt in its decadent forms in the chaotic times that lie ahead. The purpose of the meditations prescribed by Ignatius Loyola[2] and which are faithfully observed by Jesuits is to make the Jesuit first and foremost a soldier of the generalissimo Jesus Christ.

Here are a few samples. Let us take, for example, the spiritual exercise of the second week. The exercitant must always begin with a preliminary meditation in which he evokes in imagination 'the Kingdom of Christ'. He must visualize this Kingdom with Christ as supreme commander in the vanguard leading his legions, whose mission is to conquer the world. Then follows a preliminary prayer; then the first preamble.

'1. It consists in a clear representation of the place; here I must see with the eyes of imagination the synagogues, towns and villages which Christ our Lord passed through on His mission.'

All this must be visualized in a complete picture so that the novice sees the situation and all the separate representations as something which is visibly present to him.

'2. I ask for the grace which I desire. Here I must ask of our Lord the grace that I should not be deaf to His call, but should be prompt and diligent to fulfil His most holy will.'

## Lecture VIII

Then follows the actual exercise. (What I have quoted so far were preparatory exercises.) The first part again includes several points. The soul is very carefully prepared.

'Point 1. I conjure up a picture of a terrestrial King chosen by God our Lord Himself to whom all Christians and all princes render homage and obedience.'

The exercitant must hold this before him in his imagination with the same intensity as a sensory representation.

'Point 2. I observe how the King addresses all his subjects and says to them: "It is my will to conquer all the territories of the infidels. Therefore whosoever would go forth with me must be content with the same food as myself, the same drink and clothing, etcetera. He must also toil with me by day and keep watch with me by night so that he may share in the victory with me, even as he shared in the toil." '

This strengthens the will, in that sensible images penetrate directly into this will, illuminate it and spiritualize it.

'Point 3. I consider how his faithful subjects must answer a King so kind and so generous, and consequently how the man who would refuse the appeal of such a King would be deserving of censure by the whole world and would be regarded as an ignoble Knight.'

The exercitant must clearly recognize that if he is not a true soldier, a warrior of this generalissimo, then the whole world will look upon him as unworthy.

Then follows the second part of this exercise of the 'second week.'

'The second part of this exercise consists in applying the previous example of the terrestrial King to Christ our Lord in accordance with the three points mentioned above.

'Point 1. If we regard an appeal of the terrestrial King to his subjects as deserving of our consideration, then how much more deserving of our consideration is it to see Christ our Lord, the Eternal King, and the whole world assembled before Him, to see how He appeals to all and each one in particular saying: "It is my will to conquer the whole world and to subjugate my enemies and thus enter into the glory of my Father. Whoever therefore will follow me must be prepared to labour with me, so that, by following me in suffering, he may also follow me in glory."

'Point 2 To consider that all who are endowed with judgement and reason will offer themselves entirely for this arduous service.

'Point 3. Those who are animated by the desire to show still greater devotion and to distinguish themselves in the total service of their eternal King and universal Lord will not only offer themselves wholly for such arduous service, but will also fight against their own sensuality, their carnal lusts and their attachment to the world and thus make sacrifices of higher value and greater importance, saying:

' "Eternal Lord of all things, with Thy favour and help, in the presence of Thy infinite Goodness and of Thy glorious Mother and of all the saints of the heavenly Court, I present my body as a living sacrifice and swear that it is my wish and desire and my firm resolve, provided it is for Thy greater service and praise, to imitate Thee in enduring all injustice, all humiliation and all poverty, both actual and spiritual, if it shall please Thy most holy Majesty to choose me and admit me to this life and to this state."

'This exercise should be practised twice a day, in the morning on rising and one hour before lunch or dinner.

'For the second week and the following weeks it is very beneficial at times to read passages from *The Imitation of Christ* or from the Gospels and lives of the Saints.'

to be read in conjunction with those meditations which train especially the will through visualization. One must know how the will develops when it is under the influence of these Imaginations—this martial will in the realm of the

## Lecture VIII

Spirit which makes Christ Jesus its generalissimo! The exercise speaks of the 'heavenly Court which one serves in all forms of submission and humility'. With these exercises, which through the imagination train especially the will, is associated something which exercises a powerful influence upon the will when it is continually repeated. For the schooling of Jesuits is above all a schooling of the will. It is recommended to repeat daily the above meditation in the following weeks as a basic meditation and where possible in the same form, before the selected daily meditation, before the 'contemplation'. Let us take, for example, the fourth day. We have the normal preliminary prayer then a first preamble.

'1. We visualize the historical event—Christ summons and assembles all men under His standard, and Lucifer, on the other hand, under his standard.'

One must have an exact visual picture of the standard. And one must also visualize two armies, each preceded by its standard, the standard of Lucifer and the standard of Christ.

'2. You form a clear picture of the place; here a vast plain round about Jerusalem, where stands Christ our Lord, the sole and supreme commander of the just and good, with His army in battle order; and another plain round about Babylon where stands Lucifer, chief of the enemy forces.'

The two armies now face each other—the standard of Lucifer and the standard of Christ.

'3. I ask for what I desire: here I ask for knowledge of the lures of the evil adversary and for help to preserve myself from them; also for knowledge of the true life of which our sovereign and true commander is the exemplar, and for grace to imitate Him.'

Now follows the first part of the actual exercise: the standard of Lucifer; the exercitant therefore directs his spiritual eye of imagination upon the army which follows the standard of Lucifer.

'Point 1. Imagine you see the chief of all the adversaries in the vast plain around Babylon seated on a high throne of fire and smoke, a figure inspiring terror and fear.

'Point 2. Consider how he summons innumerable demons, scattering them abroad, some to one city, some to another and thus over the whole earth without overlooking any province, place, station in life or any single individual.'

This despatch of demons must be visualized concretely and in detail.

'Point 3. Consider the address he makes to them, how he enjoins upon them to prepare snares and fetters to bind men. First, they are to tempt men to covet riches, as he (Lucifer) is accustomed to do in most cases, so that they may the more easily attain the vain approbation of the world and then develop an overweening pride.

'Accordingly, the first step will be riches, the second fame, the third pride. And from these three steps Lucifer seduces man to all the other vices.'

## Second Part. The standard of Christ

'In the same way we must picture to ourselves on the opposing side, the sovereign and true commander, Christ our Lord.

'Point 1. Consider Christ our Lord, beautiful and gracious to behold, standing in a lowly place, in a vast plain about the region of Jerusalem.

'Point 2. Consider how the Lord of the whole world chooses so many persons, apostles, disciples, etcetera, and sends them forth into all lands to preach the Gospel to men of all stations in life and of every condition.

'Point 3. Consider the address which Christ our Lord

## Lecture VIII

holds in the presence of all His servants and friends whom He sends on this crusade, recommending them to endeavour to help all, first urging upon them to accept the highest spiritual poverty, and, if it should find favour in the eyes of His divine Majesty and if, should he deign to choose them, to accept also actual poverty; secondly to desire humiliation and contempt, for from these two things, poverty and humiliation, springs humility.

'Accordingly there are three steps: first, poverty as opposed to riches, secondly, humiliation and contempt as opposed to worldly fame, thirdly, humility as opposed to pride. And from these three steps the ambassadors of Christ shall lead men to the other virtues.'

The spiritual exercises are practised in this way. As I have already said, what matters is that a temporal kingdom, and organized as such, must be represented as the army of Christ Jesus. Jesuitism is the most consistent, the best, and moreover extremely well organized expression, of what I referred to as the second current—the impulse of the People of the Church. We shall find in effect that fundamentally this impulse of the People of the Church is to reduce the unique revelation which occurred at Jerusalem to the level of a temporal Kingdom. For the end and object of the exercises is ultimately to bring the exercitant to choose himself as soldier serving under the banner of Christ and to feel himself to be a true soldier of Christ. That was the message entrusted to Ignatius Loyola through a revelation of a special kind. He first performed heroic deeds as a soldier, then as he lay on a sick bed recovering from his wounds was led as a result of meditations (I will not say by what power) to transform the martial impulse which formerly inspired him into the impulse to become a soldier of Christ. It is one of the most interesting phenomena of world history to observe how the martial qualities of an outstandingly brave soldier are transformed through meditations into spiritual qualities.

Where the continuous influence which the Christ impulse had exercised within the People of the Christ had been blunted, it is clear that Jesuitism had to assume this extreme form. And the question arises: is there not another form of Christianity diametrically opposed to that of Jesuitism? In that event a force would have to emerge in the territory occupied by the People of the Church. From the different reactions of Lutheranism, Zwinglianism,[3] Calvinism, Schwenkfeldism and the Anabaptists, from this chaos and fragmentation, a force would have to emerge which not only follows the line of Jesuit thought (for Jesuitism is only an extreme expression of Catholic dogma)—but which is diametrically opposed to Jesuitism, something which seeks to break away from this community of the People of the Church, whilst Jesuitism seeks to be ever more deeply involved in it. Jesuitism wishes to transform the Christ impulse into a purely temporal sovereignty, to found a terrestrial state which is at the same time a Jesuit state, and which is governed in accordance with the principles of those who have volunteered to become soldiers of the generalissimo Christ. What could be the force which is the antithesis of Jesuitism?

The counter-impulse would be that which seeks, not to materialize the spiritual, but to spiritualize the material world. This impulse is a natural endowment amongst the true People of the Christ and finds expression in Solovieff[4] though often tentatively. Within the territory of the true People of the Church there exists something which is radically opposed to Jesuitism, something which rejects any direct intervention of the spiritual in power politics and external affairs, and wishes the Christ impulse to penetrate into the souls of men, and indirectly through these souls to operate in the external world. Such an impulse might well appear in

## Lecture VIII

the People of the Church—because, in the meantime, much might tend in this direction; but it would seek to direct evolution in such a way that the spiritual Christ impulse penetrates only into the souls and remains to some extent esoteric, esoteric in the best and noblest sense of the term. Whilst Jesuitism wishes to tranform everything into a temporal kingdom, this other current would simply regard the temporal kingdom as something which, if need be, must exist on the physical plane, something, however, which unites men so that they can lift up their souls to higher realms. This current which is the polar opposite of Jesuitism is Goetheanism.

The aim of Goetheanism is the exact opposite of that of Jesuitism. And you will understand Goetheanism from a different angle if you consider it as by nature diametrically opposed to Jesuitism. That is why Jesuitism is, and ever will be the sworn foe of Goetheanism. They cannot coexist; they know each other too well and Jesuitism is well informed on Goethe. The best book on Goethe, from the Jesuit standpoint of course, is that of the Jesuit father, Baumgartner.[5] What the various German professors and the Englishman, G. H. Lewes[6], have written about Goethe is pure dilettantism compared with the three volumes by Baumgartner. He knows what he is about! As an adversary he sees Goethe with a more critical eye. Nor does he write like a German professor of average intelligence or like the Englishman, Lewes, who depicts a man who was indeed born in Frankfurt in 1749; he is said to have lived through the same experiences as Goethe, but the man he depicts is not Goethe. But Baumgartner's portrait is reinforced with the forces of will derived from his meditations. Thus Goetheanism, which is destined to play a part in the future, is linked to something which is directly associated with the epoch beginning with the fifteenth century and leading via the Reformation to Jesuitism.

I will discuss the third current tomorrow. I have described to you today the People of the Christ, the People of the Church and the third current which interpenetrates them and then the reciprocal action of these currents, in order to give you an insight into recent religious developments through a study of their symptoms. I will say more of this tomorrow.

## LECTURE IX

Let us resume our observations of yesterday. I showed how, in the main, through factors I have mentioned, the People of the Christ was diverted eastwards and how, as a consequence of other factors, the Peoples of the Church developed in the centre of Europe and spread from there in a westward direction. I then pointed out how the various conflicts which arose at the turning-point which marked the beginning of the fifth post-Atlantean epoch were connected with this basic fact. I also showed how, within that territory where the true People of the Church developed, through the fact that the Christ impulse to some extent no longer exercised a lasting influence, but was associated with a definite moment in time and had to be transmitted through tradition and written records, there arose the troubled relationship between Christianity and the politically organized church, subject to the Roman pontiff; and how then other individual churches submitted to Rome. These other churches, though manifesting considerable differences from the papal church have, however, many features in common with it—in any case certain things which are of interest to us in this context and which seem to indicate that the state church of the Protestants is closer to the Roman Catholic Church than to the Russian Orthodox Church, in which however the dependence of the church upon the state was never the essential factor. What was of paramount importance in the Russian church was the way in which the Christ impulse, in unbroken activity, expressed itself through the Russian people. I then showed how the radical consequence of this dragging down of the Christ impulse into purely worldly affairs was the establishment of Jesuitism, and how Goetheanism\* appeared as the antithesis of Jesuitism.

This Goetheanism endeavours to promote a countermovement, somewhat akin to Russian Christianity. It seeks to spiritualize that which exists here on the physical plane, so that, despite the circumstances on the physical plane, the soul unites with the impulses which sustain the spiritual world itself, impulses which are not brought down directly to the plane of sensible reality, as in Jesuitism, but are mediated by the soul. As was his custom, Goethe seldom expressed his most intimate thoughts on this subject. But if we wish to know them we must again refer to that passage in Wilhelm Meister to which I have already drawn attention in another context. It is the passage where Wilhelm Meister enters Jarno's castle and is shown a picture gallery depicting world history, and in the framework of this world history the religious evolution of mankind. Wilhelm Meister is led by the guide to a picture where history is portrayed as ending with the destruction of Jerusalem. He drew the attention of the guide to the absence of any representation of the Divine Being who had been active in Palestine immediately before the destruction of Jerusalem. Wilhelm was then led into a second gallery where he was shown what was missing in the first gallery—the life of Christ up to the Last Supper. And it was explained to him that all the different religions represented in the first gallery up to the time of the destruction of Jerusalem were related to the human being in so far as he was a member of an ethnic group. All these scenes represented an ethnic or folk religion. What he had seen in the second gallery, however, was related to the individual, was addressed to the individual; it was a personal and private matter. It could only be revealed to the

\* See also *Goethestudien und Goetheanische Denkmethoden* (in Bibl. Nr. 36).

## Lecture IX

individual, it could not be an ethnic religion for it was addressed to the human being, to the individual as such.

Wilhelm Meister then remarked that he still missed here, i.e. in the second gallery, the story of Christ Jesus from the time of the Last Supper until His Death and Ascension. He was then led to a third and highly secret gallery where these scenes were represented. But at the same time the guide pointed out to him that these representations were a matter of such intimacy that one had no right to portray them in the profane fashion in which they were usually presented to the public. They must appeal to the innermost being of man.

Now one can claim with good reason that what was still valid in Goethe's day, namely, that the representation of the Passion of Christ Jesus should be withheld from the public, no longer applies today. Since that time we have passed through many stages of development. But I should like to point out that Goethe's whole attitude to this question is revealed in this passage from Wilhelm Meister. Goethe shows quite clearly that he wishes the Christ impulse to penetrate into the inmost recesses of the soul; he wishes to dissociate it from the national impulse, from the national state. He wishes to establish a direct relationship between the individual soul and the Christ impulse. This is extremely important for an understanding not only of Goethe, but of Goetheanism. For, as I said recently, in relation to external culture, Goethe and the whole of Goetheanism are in reality isolated, but when one bears in mind the more inward religious development of civilized mankind one cannot say the same of the progress of evolution. Goethe, for his part, represents in a certain respect the continuation of something else. But in order to understand how Goethe is to some extent opposed to everything that is usually manifested in the Church of Central Europe, we must now consider a third impulse.

*From Symptom to Reality in Modern History*

This third impulse is localized more to the West, and to a certain extent is the driving force behind the nations—one cannot say that it inspires them. That which emerged in its extreme form as Jesuitism, as the militia of the generalissimo Jesus Christ, is deeply rooted in the very nature of the civilized world. In order to understand this we must turn our attention to the controversy dating back to the fourth century which was felt long afterwards. From your knowledge of the history of religions you will recall that, in its triumphal march from East to West, Christianity assumed divers forms and amongst them those of Arianism and Athanasianism. The peoples—Goths, Langobards and Franks—who took part in what is mistakenly called the migration of nations were originally Arians.

Now the doctrinal conflict between the Arians and Athanasians[1] is probably of little interest to you today, but it played a certain part and we must return to it. It arose from a conflict between Arius and Athanasius which began at Alexandria and was given new impetus in Antioch. Athanasius maintained that Christ is a God, like God the Father, that a Father-God therefore exists and that Christ is of the same nature and substance as the Father from all eternity. This doctrine passed over into Roman Catholicism which still professes today the faith of Athanasius. Thus at the root of Roman Catholicism is the belief that the Son is eternal and of the same nature and substance as the Father.

Arius opposed this view. He held that there was a supreme God, the Father, and that the Divine Son, i.e. Christ, was begotten of the Father before all ages. He was a separate being from the Father, different in substance and nature, the perfect creature who is nearer to man than the Father, the mediator between the Creator, who is beyond the reach of human understanding, and the creature.

Strange as it may seem this appears at first sight to be a

## Lecture IX

doctrinal dispute. But it is a doctrinal dispute only in the eyes of modern man. In the first centuries of Christianity it had deeper implications, for Arian Christianity, based on the relationship between the Son and the Father, as I have just indicated, was something natural and self-evident to the Goths and Langobards—all those peoples who first took over from Rome after the fall of the empire. Instinctively they were Arians. Ulfilas's translation of the Bible[2] shows quite clearly that he was an adherent of Arius. The Goths and Langobards[2] who invaded Italy were also Arians, and only when Clovis[2] was converted to Christianity did the Franks accept Christianity. They adopted somewhat superficially the doctrine of Athanasius which was foreign to their nature, for they had formerly been Arians at heart. And when Christianity hoisted its banner under the leadership of Charles the Great[2] everyone was instructed in the creed of Athanasius. Thus the ground was prepared for the transition to the Church of Rome. A large part of the barbarian peoples, Goths, Langobards, etcetera, perished; the ethnic remnants who survived were driven out or annihilated by the Athanasians. Arianism lived on in the form of sects; but as a tribal religion it ceased to be an active force.

Two questions now arise: first, what distinguishes Arianism from Athanasianism? Secondly, why did Arianism disappear from the stage of European history, at least as far as any visible symptoms are concerned? Arianism is the last offshoot of those conceptions of the world which, when they aspired to the divine, still sought to find a relation between the sensible world and the divine-spiritual, and which still felt the need to unite the sense-perceptible with the divine-spiritual. In Arianism we find in a somewhat more abstract form the same impulse that we find in the Christ impulse of Russia—but only as impulse, not in the form of sacramentalism and cultus. This form of the Christ impulse had to be

207

abandoned because it was unsuited to the peoples of Europe. And it was also extirpated by the Athanasians for the same reason.

In order to have a clearer understanding of these questions we must consider what was the original constitution of soul of the different peoples of Europe. The original psychic make-up of the peoples who took over from the Roman Empire, who, it is said, invaded and settled in its territory (which is not strictly true, but I have not the time at present to rectify this misconception), the psychic disposition of the so-called Teutonic peoples was originally of a different nature. These peoples came from widely different directions and mingled with an autochthonous population of Europe which is rightly called the Celtic population. Vestiges of this Celtic population can still be found here and there amongst certain ethnic groups. Today when there is a wish to preserve national identity, people are intent upon preserving at all costs the Celtic element wherever they find it, or imagine they have found it. In order to form a true picture of the national or folk element in Europe we must imagine a proto-European culture, a Celtic culture, within which the other cultures developed—the Teutonic, the Romanic (i.e. of the Romance peoples), the Anglo-Saxons, etcetera.

The Celtic element has survived longest in its original form in the British Isles, especially in Wales. It is there that it has retained longest its original character. And just as a certain kind of religious sentiment had been diverted towards the East, with the result that the Russian people became the People of the Christ, so too, by virtue of certain facts which you can verify in any text-book of history a certain impulse emanated in the West from the British Isles. It is this impulse, an echo of the original Celtism, which ultimately determined the form of the religious life in the West, just as

## Lecture IX

other influences determined that of the East and Central Europe.

Now in order to understand these events we must consider the question: what kind of people were the Celts? Though widely differentiated in many respects, they had one feature in common—they showed little interest in the relationship between nature and mankind. They imagined man as insulated from nature. They were interested in everything pertaining to man, but they had no interest in the way in which man is related to nature, how man is an integral part of nature. Whilst in the East, for example, in direct contrast to Celtism, one always feels profoundly the relation between man and nature, that man is to some extent a product of nature, as I showed in the case of Goethe, the Celt, on the other hand, had little understanding for the relationship between human nature and cosmic nature. He had a strong sense for a common way of life, for community life. But amongst the ancient Celts this corporate life was organized on the authoritarian principle of leaders and subordinates, those who commanded and those who obeyed. Essentially its structure was aristrocratic, anti-democratic, and in Europe this can be traced to Celtic antiquity. It was an organization based on aristocracy and this was its fundamental character.

Now there was a time when this aristocratic, Celtic, monarchical element flourished. The king as leader surrounded by his vassals, etcetera, this is a product of Celtism. And the last of such leaders who, in his own interests, still relied upon the original Celtic impulses was King Arthur with his Round Table in Wales. Arthur with his twelve Knights whose duty, so it is recorded—though this should not be taken literally—was to slay monsters and overcome demons. All this bears witness to the time of man's union with the spiritual world. The manner in which the Arthurian legend sprang up, the many legends associated with King Arthur, all this shows that the Celtic element lived on in the monarchical principle. Hence the readiness to accept commands, injunctions and direction from the King.

Now the Christ of Ulfilas, the Christ of the Goths was strongly impregnated with Arianism. He was a Christ for all men, for those who, in a certain sense, felt themselves as equals, who accepted no class differences, no claims to aristocracy. At the same time he was a last echo of that instinctive feeling in the East for the communion between man and the cosmos, between man and nature. Nature was to some extent excluded from the social structure of the Celtic monarchical system.

These two streams converged first of all in Europe (I cannot now enter into details, I can only discuss the main features). Then they were joined to a third stream. As a result of this confluence Arianism at first gained ground; but since it was a survival of a conception that linked nature and man, it was not understood by those who, as heirs of the Teutonic and Frankish peoples, were still influenced by purely Celtic impulses. They understood only a monarchical system such as their own. And therefore the need arose, still perceptible in the Old Saxon religious epic *Heliand*[2], to portray the Christ as a royal commander, a sovereign chief, as a feudal lord with his liege men. This reinterpretation of the Christ as a royal commander stemmed from the inability to understand what came over from the East and from the need to venerate Christ as both a spiritual and temporal King.

The third stream came from the South, from the Roman Empire. It had already been infected earlier with what one might perhaps call today the bureaucratic mentality. The Roman Empire—(it was not a state; it could best be described as a structure akin to a state) is very like—but different, in

## Lecture IX

that the different territories are geographically remote from each other and different conditions determine the social structure—this Roman Empire is very like what emerged from the monarchical system though starting from different principles. Formerly a republic, it developed into an imperial organization, into an empire akin to what developed out of the various kingdoms of the Celtic civilization, but with a Teutonic flavouring.

Now the intellectual and emotional attitude towards social life which originated in the South, in the Roman Empire—because it envisaged an external structure on the physical plane—could never really find any common ground with Arianism which still survived as an old instinctive impulse from the East. This Roman impulse needed, paradoxically, something that was incomprehensible, something that had to be decreed. And as kings and emperors governed by decree, so too the Papacy. The doctrine of Athanasius could be brought home to mankind by appealing to certain feelings which were especially developed in the peoples I have mentioned; after all, these sentiments exist in everyone to some extent. The faith professed by Athanasius contains little that appeals to human feeling or understanding; if it is to be incorporated in the community it must be imposed by decree, it must have the sanction of law after the fashion of secular laws. And so it came to pass: the strange incomprehensible doctrine of the identity of the Father and the Son, who are co-equal and co-eternal, was later understood to imply that this doctrine transcended human logic; it must become an article of faith. It is something that can be decreed. The Athanasian faith can be imposed by decree. And since it was directly dependent upon authoritarian directives it could be introduced into an ecclesiastical organization with political leanings. Arianism, on the other hand, appealed to the individual; it could not be incorporated in an ecclesiastical organization, nor be imposed by decree. But authoritarian directives were important for the reasons I have mentioned.

Thus that which came from the south, from Athanasianism with its authoritarian tendency, merged with an instinctive need for an organization directed by a leader with twelve subordinates. In Central Europe these elements are interwoven. In Western Europe, in the British Isles and later also in America, there survived however a certain remnant of the old aristocratic outlook such as existed in the feudal nobility, in the old aristocracy, in that element which is responsible for the social structure and introduces the spiritual into the social life. That the spiritual element was regarded as an integral part of the social life is evident from the Arthurian legend which relates that it was the duty of the Knights of the Round Table to slay monsters and to wage war on demons. The spiritual therefore is operative here; it can only be cultivated if it is not imposed by decree, but is a spontaneous expression and is consciously directed. Thus, whilst the People of the Church developed in Central Europe there arose in the West, especially amongst the English-speaking peoples, what may be called the 'People of the Lodges', to give a name to this third stream. In the West there had existed originally a tendency to form societies, to promote in these societies a spirit of organization. But in the final analysis an organization is only of value if it is created imperceptibly by spiritual means, otherwise it must be imposed by decree. And this is what happened in Central Europe; it was more in the society which later developed as a continuation of Celtism, in the English-speaking peoples, that attempts were made to rule in conformity with the lodges. Thus arose the 'People or Peoples of the Lodges' whose conspicuous feature is not the organization of man-

## Lecture IX

kind as a whole, but rather the division of mankind into separate groups and orders.

The division into orders stems from this continuation of the feudal element which is associated with the legend of King Arthur. In history things are interwoven. One can never understand a new development if one imagines that the effect follows directly from the cause. In the course of development things interpenetrate. And it is a strange fact that, in relation to its mode of representation and to everything that is active in the human soul, the principle of the lodges (of which freemasonry is a grotesque caricature) is inwardly related to Jesuitism. Though Jesuitism is bitterly hostile to the lodges, there is nevertheless great similarity in their mode of representation. And a Celtic streak in Ignatius Loyola certainly contributed to his consummate achievement.

In the East therefore the People of the Christ arose; they were the bearer of the continuous Christ impulse. For the man of the East accepts as a matter of course that throughout his life he receives the continuous influx of the Christ impulse. For the People of the Christ in Central Europe this impulse has become blunted or emasculated because it has been associated with a unique event at the beginning of our era and was later supplemented by the promulgation of decrees, state decrees, and by traditional transmission in conformity with Catholic doctrine. In the West, in the system of the Lodges, the Christ impulse was at first very much in question and so became still further emasculated. Thus the modes of thinking which really originate in this lodge impulse, which stems from Celtism and is a last echo of Celtism, gave birth to deism and what is called modern *Aufklärung*.[3] It is extremely interesting to see the vast difference between the attitude of a member of the People of the Church in Central Europe to the Christ impulse and that of a citizen of the British Empire. But I must ask you not to judge this difference of attitude by the isolated individual, for obviously the impulse of the Church has spread also to England and one must accept things as they are in reality; one must take into account those people who are associated with what I have described as the lodge impulse which has invaded the state administration especially in the whole of the West.

The question is: What then is the relationship of the member of the People of the Christ to Christ? He knows that when he is really at one with himself he finds the Christ impulse—for this impulse is present in his soul and is continuously active in his soul. The member of the People of the Church speaks, perhaps, like Augustine who, at the age of maturity, in answer to the question, how do I find the Christ? replied: 'The Church tells me who is the Christ. I can learn it from the Church, for the Church has preserved in its tradition the original teaching about the Christ.'—He who belongs to the People of the Lodges—I mean the true member of the Lodges—has a different approach to the Christ from the People of the Church and the People of the Christ. He says to himself: history speaks of a Christ who once existed. Is it reasonable to believe in such a Christ? How can the influence of Christ be justified historically before the bar of reason? This, fundamentally, is the Christology of the *Aufklärung* which demands that the Christ be vindicated by reason.

Now in order to understand what is involved here we must be quite clear that it is possible to know God without the inspiration of the Christ impulse. One need only be slightly mentally abnormal—just as the atheist is a person who is physically ill in some respect—to arrive at the idea of God or admit the existence of God by way of speculation or of mysticism. For deism is the fundamental belief of *Aufklärung*.

## Lecture IX

One arrives directly at the belief of the *Aufklärung* that a God exists.

Now for those who are heirs of the People of the Lodges it is a question of finding a rational justification for the existence of Christ alongside the universal God. Amongst the various personalities characteristic of this rational approach I have selected Herbert of Cherbury[4] who died in 1648, the year of the peace of Westphalia. He attempted to find a rational justification for the Christ impulse. A true member of the Russian people, for example, i.e. of the People of the Christ, would find a rational approach to the Christ impulse unthinkable. That would be tantamount to demanding of him to justify the presence of his head upon his shoulders. One possesses a head—and equally surely one possesses the Christ impulse. What people such as Cherbury want to know is something different: is it reasonable to accept alongside the God, to the idea of whom enlightened thinking leads, the existence of a Christ? One must first study man from a rational point of view in order to find a justification for this approach.

Not every member of the People of the Lodges of course responds in this way! The philosophers express their views in definite, clear-cut concepts; but others are not given to reflection; but all those who are in any way connected with the impulse of the Peoples of the Lodges, instinctively, emotionally and in the conclusions they unconsciously draw, adopt this rational approach. Cherbury started from an examination of the common factor in the different religions. Now this is a typical trick of the *Aufklärung*. Since they themselves cannot arrive at the spirit, at least as far as the Christ impulse is concerned, but only at the abstract notion of the god of deism, they ask: is it natural for man to discover this or that? Cherbury, who had travelled widely, endeavoured first of all to discover the common factor in the different religions. He found that they had a great deal in common and he tried to summarize these common factors in five propositions. These five propositions are most important and we must examine them closely.

The first proposition states: *A God exists.* Since the various peoples belonging to widely differing religions instinctively admit the existence of a God, he finds it natural therefore to admit that a God exists.

Secondly: *The God demands veneration.* Again a common feature of all religions.

Thirdly: *This veneration must consist in virtue and piety.*

Fourthly: *There must be repentence and expiation of sins.*

Fifthly: *In the hereafter there is a justice that rewards and punishes.*

As you see, there is no mention of the Christ impulse. But in these five propositions one finds the most one can know when one relies only upon the religious impulse emanating from the lodges. *Aufklärung* is a further development of this way of looking at things. Hobbes,[5] Locke[5] and others constantly raised the question: since there is a tradition which speaks of Jesus Christ, is it reasonable to believe in His existence? And finally they are prepared to say: what is written in the Gospels, what is handed down by tradition on the subject of Christ Jesus agrees with the fundamental tenets common to all religions. It seems that the Christ wished to collate the common factors in all religions, that a divinely inspired personality (this can be envisaged more or less) had once existed who taught what is best in all religions. The *Aufklärer* found this to be reasonable. And Tindal who lived from 1647–1733 wrote a book entitled *Christianity as Old as Creation*. This book is very important for it gives us an insight into the nature of *Aufklärung* which was subsequently diluted by Voltaireism etcetera. Tindal wanted to show that in reality all men, the more enlightened men, have always

## Lecture IX

been Christians, and that Christ simply embodied the best in all religions.

Thus the Christ is reduced to the status of a teacher: whether we call Him Messiah or Master, or what you will, He is nothing more than a teacher. It is not so much the fact of the Christ that is important, but that He exists and dwells amongst us, that He offers a religious teaching embodying the most precious element, the element which is common to the religions of the rest of mankind.

The idea I have just expressed may of course assume widely different forms, but the basic form persists—the Christ is teacher. When we consider the typical representatives of the People of the Christ, the People of the Church and the People of the Lodges, representatives who show wide variations, when we seek the reality behind the appearance, then we can say that for the People of the Christ: Christ is Spirit and therefore He is in no way concerned with any institutions on the physical plane. But the mystery of His incarnation remains. For the People of the Church: Christ is King, a conception which may assume various nuances. And this conception lives on also in the People of the Lodges, but in its further development it is modified and becomes: Christ is the Teacher.

We must bear in mind these different aspects of the European consciousness for they are deeply rooted not only in the individual, but also in what has developed spiritually in Europe in the fifth post-Atlantean epoch and also in many of the social forms. They are the principal nuances assumed by the Christ impulse. Much more could be said on this subject; I can only give a brief outline today since my time is short.

Let us now return to the three forms of evolution of which I spoke yesterday. In its present stage of development the whole of mankind is now living in the Sentient Soul, corresponding to the age of twenty-eight to twenty-one in man. Every single man, qua individual, develops the Consciousness Soul today in the course of the post-Atlantean epoch. Finally a third evolution unfolds within the folk-souls of which I spoke yesterday. We have, on the one hand, the historical facts and the influence they exert, and on the other hand the folk-souls with their different religious nuances. As a result of this interaction, for the People of the Christ: Christ is the Spirit; for the People of the Church: Christ is the King; for the People of the Lodges: Christ is the Teacher. These different responses are determined by the different folk characteristics. That is the third evolution.

In external reality things always interpenetrate—they work upon each other and through each other. If you ask who is representative of the People of the Lodges, of the deism of the *Aufklärung* then, strangely enough, a perfect example is Harnack[6] in Berlin! He is a much more representative example than anyone on the other side of the Channel. In modern life things are much confused. If we wish to understand events and trace them back to their origin we must look beyond externalities. We must be quite clear that the third stream of evolution which is linked to the national element is connected with what I have described here. But because of the presence of the other evolutionary currents a reaction always follows, the assault of the Consciousness Soul upon this national element, and this assault manifests itself at divers points. It starts from different centres. And one of these waves of assault is Goetheanism which, in reality, has nothing to do with what I have just described, and yet, when considered from a particular angle, is closely related to it. Parallel with the Arthurian current there developed early on the Grail current which is the antithesis of the Arthurian current. He who wishes to

## Lecture IX

visit the Temple of the Grail must follow dangerous and almost inaccessible paths for sixty miles. The Temple lies remote and well concealed; one learns nothing there unless one asks. In brief, the purpose of this whole Grail impulse is to restore the link between the inmost core of the human soul (where the Consciousness Soul awakens) and the spiritual world. It is (if I may say so) an attempt artificially to lift up the sensible world to the spiritual world which is instinctive in the People of the Christ. The following diagram shows this strange interpenetration of the religious impulses

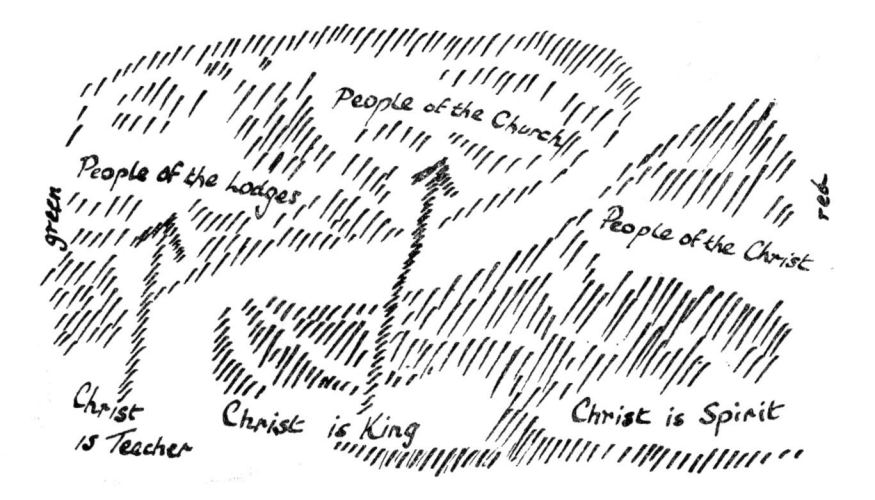

*People of the Church*
*People of the Lodges* (green) — *People of the Christ* (red)
*Christ is Teacher* — *Christ is King* — *Christ is Spirit*

of Europe. We have here an impulse which still exists today instinctively, in embryo and undeveloped, in the People of the Christ (red); philosophic spirits such as Solovieff come to accept this Christ impulse as something self-evident.

On account of its ethnographical and ethnic situation, Central Europe is not disposed to accept the Christ impulse as something self-evident; it had to be imposed artificially. And so we have an intervention of the current of the Grail radiating in the direction of Europe—a Grail current that is not limited therefore to the folk element. This Grail atmosphere was active in Goethe, in the depths of his subconscious. If you look for this Grail atmosphere you will find it everywhere. Goethe is not an isolated phenomenon in this respect and therefore he is linked with what preceded him in the West. He has nothing in common with Luther, German mysticism and its forerunners; this was in part a formative influence and helped to shape him as a man of culture. It is the Grail atmosphere which leads him to distinguish three stages in man's relation to religion: first the religion of the people; secondly, the religion of the philosophers portrayed in the second gallery, and finally the most intimate religion in the third gallery, the religion which touches the inmost depths of the soul and embraces the mysteries of death and resurrection. It is the Grail atmosphere which inspires him to exalt the religious impulse active in the sensible world and not to drag it down after the fashion of the Jesuits. And paradoxical as it may seem today the Grail atmosphere is found today in Russia. And the future role that the Russian soul will play in the sixth post-Atlantean epoch depends upon this unconquerable spirit of the Grail in the Russian people.

So much for the one side. Let us now consider the other side. Here we have those who regard the Christ impulse neither as an inspiration, as in the East, nor as a living force transmitted by tradition and the Scriptures, but as something rational. It is in this form that it spread within the Lodges and their ramifications. (In the diagram I indicate this by the colour green.) Later it became politicized in the West and is the last offshoot of the Arthurian current. And just as the Christ impulse in the Russian people is continued in the Grail quest and irradiates all men of good will in the West, so the other current penetrates into all members of the

## Lecture IX

People of the Church and takes on the particular colouring of Jesuitism. That the Jesuits are the sworn enemy of that which emanates from the Lodges is not important: anyone and anything can be the declared enemy of the outlook of the Lodges. It is a historical fact that the Jesuits have not only infiltrated the Lodges, that high-ranking Jesuits are in contact with the high dignitaries of the Lodges, but that both, though active in different peoples, have a common root, though the one gave birth to the Papacy, the other to freedom, rationalism, to the *Aufklärung*. I have now given you a kind of picture of what may be called the working of the evolution of the Consciousness Soul. I described to you earlier the three stages of evolution proceeding from the East to the West which are based on the ethnic element. That they assumed the form of *Aufklärung* in the West, as a consequence of interaction, is due to the fact that every individual is involved in the evolution of the Consciousness Soul.

Then we have a third current of evolution in which the whole of mankind is involved and by virtue of which mankind ceases to develop physically at an ever earlier age. Today mankind as a whole is at the 'age' of the Sentient Soul, i.e. between the ages of twenty-eight and twenty-one. This applies to the whole of mankind.

In describing the first current, the ethnic current when folk or tribal religions arise within Christianity such as the religion of the Christ, the religion of the Church and the religion of the Lodges, we are speaking from the standpoint of the evolution of peoples (or nations) which I usually characterize as follows: the Italian peoples = the Sentient Soul; the French peoples = the Intellectual or Mind Soul, etcetera. We have described how the Consciousness Soul develops in every individual in the course of the fifth post-Atlantean epoch. In this consciousness we have the element that streams into religion. But from that moment begins the interaction with the other current, with the evolution of the Sentient Soul (common to all men) which follows a parallel course and is a far more unconscious process than that of the evolution of the Consciousness Soul.

If you study how a man like Goethe—though the impulses are often subconscious—nevertheless determines consciously his religious orientation, you see the working of the Consciousness Soul. But at the same time another element is at work in modern mankind, an element which finds powerful expression in the instinctive life, in unconscious impulses, and is intimately associated with the evolution of the Sentient Soul. And this is the trend towards socialism which is now in its early stages and will end in the way I have described. The initial impetus, it is true, is always given by the Consciousness Soul (as I have already indicated); but the development of socialism is the mission of the fifth post-Atlantean epoch and will end in the fourth millennium when it will have fulfilled its purpose. This is owing to the fact that mankind collectively is at the age of the Sentient Soul, corresponding to the age of twenty-eight to twenty-one in man. Socialism is not a matter of party politics, although there are many parties within the community, within the body social. Socialism is not a party political question as such, but a movement which of necessity will gradually develop in the course of the fifth post-Atlantean epoch. And when this epoch has run its course an instinctive feeling for socialism will be found in all men in the civilized world.

In addition to the interaction of these currents in the fifth post-Atlantean epoch there is also at work that which lies in the depths of the subconscious, the desire to find the right social structure for all mankind from now until the fourth millennium. From a deeper point of view it is not in the least surprising that socialism stirs up all sorts of ideas which

## Lecture IX

could be highly dangerous when one recalls that they derive their impulses from the depths of the subconscious, that everything is in a state of ferment and that the time is still far distant before it will come into its own. But there are rumblings beneath the surface—not, it is true, in the souls of men at present, i.e. in the astral body—but in the etheric body, in the temperaments of men. And people invent theories to explain these stirrings in the temperaments of men particularly. If these theories do not explain, as does spiritual science, what lies behind maya, then these theories, whether they are the theories of Bakunin,[7] Marx, Lassalle and the like, are simply masks, disguises, veils that conceal reality. One only becomes aware of the realities when one probes deeply into human evolution as we have attempted to do in this survey. All that is now taking place (i.e. in 1918) in the external world are simply tempestuous preparations for what after all is now smouldering, one may say, not in the souls of men, but in their temperaments. You are all socialists and you are often unaware how deeply impregnated you are with socialism because it is latent in your temperament, in the subconscious. But it is only when we are aware of this fact that we overcome that nebulous and ridiculous search for self-knowledge which looks inward and finds only a *caput mortuum*, a spiritual void, an abstraction. Man is a complex being and in order to understand him we must understand the whole world. It is important to bear this in mind.

Consider from this point of view the evolution of mankind in the course of the fifth post-Atlantean epoch. First, the People of the Christ in the East with its fundamental impulse: Christ is Spirit. It is in the nature of this people to give to the world through Russianism, as if with elemental force and from historical necessity, that for which the West of Europe could only have prepared the ground. To the Russian people as such has been assigned the mission to develop the essential reality of the Grail as a religious system up to the time of the sixth post-Atlantean epoch, so that it may then become a cultural ferment for the whole world. Small wonder then that when this impulse encounters the other impulses the latter assume strange forms.

What are these other impulses? Christ is King and Christ is Teacher. One can scarcely call 'Christ is Teacher' an impulse, for, as I have already said, the Russian soul does not really understand what it means, does not understand that one can teach Christianity and not experience it in one's soul. But as for the conception 'Christ is King'—it is inseparable from the Russian people. And we now see the clash between two things which never had the slightest affinity, the clash between the impulse 'Christ is Spirit' and Czarism, an oriental caricature of the principle which seeks to establish temporal sovereignty in the domain of religion. 'Christ is King and the Czar is his representative'—here we have the association of the Western element manifested in Czarism with something that is completely alien to Czarism, something that, through the agency of the Russian folk soul, permeates the sentient life of the Russian people.

A characteristic feature of external physical reality is that those things which inwardly are often least related to each other must rub off on each other externally. Czarism and Russianism have always been strangers to each other, they never had anything in common. Those who understand the Russian nature, especially its piety, must have found the attitude to the elimination of Czarism as something self-evident when the time was ripe. But remember that this conception 'Christ is Spirit' touches the deepest springs of our being, that it is related to the highest expression of the Consciousness Soul and that, whilst socialism is smouldering beneath the surface, it collides with that which dwells in the Sentient Soul. Small wonder then that the

## Lecture IX

expansion of socialism in Eastern Europe assumes forms that are totally incomprehensible: a chaotic interplay of the culture of the Consciousness Soul and the culture of the Sentient Soul.

Much that occurs in the external world becomes clear and comprehensible if we bear in mind these inner relationships. And it is vital for mankind today and for its future evolution that it does not neglect, out of complacency or indolence, its essential task, namely, to comprehend the situation in which we now find ourselves. People have not understood this situation, nor have they attempted to understand it. Hence the chaos, the terrible catastrophe which has overtaken Europe and America. We shall not find a way out of the present catastrophic situation until men begin to see themselves as they are and to see themselves objectively in the context of present evolution and the present epoch. We cannot afford to ignore this.

That is why it is so important to me that people should realize that the Anthroposophical Movement, as I envisage it, must be associated with an awareness of the great evolutionary impulses of mankind, with the immediate demands of our time. It is tragic that the present age shows little inclination to understand and to consider the Anthroposophical *Weltanschauung* precisely from this point of view.

I should now like to round off what I said last week in connection with *The Philosophy of Freedom* by a consideration of more general points of view. From what I have said you will realize that the rise of socialism\*at the present time is a movement deeply rooted in human nature, a movement that is steadily gaining ground. For those endowed with insight the present negative reactions to the advance of socialism are simply appalling. Despite its ominous rumblings,

---

\* See *Soziale und antisoziale Triebe im Menschen*, Bern, 12th December, 1918 (in Bibl. Nr. 186).

despite its noisy claims to recognition, it is evident that socialism, this international movement which is spreading throughout the world, prefigures the future and that what we are now seeing, the creation of all kinds of national states and petty national states at the present time, is a retrograde step that inhibits the evolution of mankind. The dictum 'to every nation its national state' is a terrible obstacle to an understanding of the fifth post-Atlantean epoch. Where this will end nobody knows; but this is what people are saying! At the same time this outlook is entirely permeated with the backward forces of the Arthurian impulse, with the desire for external organization. The antithesis to this is the Grail quest which is intimately related to Goethean principles and aims at individualism, at autonomy in the domain of ethics and science; it concerns itself especially with the individual and his development and not with groups which have lost their significance today and which must be eliminated by means of international socialism because that is the trend of evolution.

And for this reason one must also say: in Goetheanism with its individualism—you will recall that I emphasized the individualism in Goethe's *Weltanschauung* in my early Goethe publications and also in my book *Goethe's Weltanschauung* when I showed that this individualism is a natural consequence of Goetheanism—in this individualism, which can only culminate in a philosophy of feedom, there lies that which of necessity must lead to the development of socialism. And so we can recognize the existence of two poles—individualism and socialism—towards which mankind tends in the fifth post-Atlantean epoch. In order to develop a right understanding of these things we must ascertain what principle must be added to socialism if socialism is to follow the true course of human evolution. The socialists of today have no idea what, of necessity, socialism entails and must

## Lecture IX

entail—the true socialism that will be achieved to some extent only in the fourth millennium if it develops in the right way. It is especially important that this socialism be developed in conjunction with a true feeling for the being of the whole man, for man as a tripartite being of body, soul and spirit. The religious impulses of the particular ethnic groups will contribute in their different ways to an understanding of this tripartite division of man. The East and the Russian people to the understanding of the spirit; the West to an understanding of the body; Central Europe to an understanding of the soul. But all these impulses are interwoven of course. They must not be systematized or classified, but within this tripartite division the real principle, the true impulse of socialism must first be developed.

The real impulse of socialism consists in the realization of fraternity in the widest sense of the term in the external structure of society. True fraternity of course has nothing to do with equality. Take the case of fraternity within the same family: where one child is seven years old and his brother is newly born there can be no question of equality. One must first understand what is meant by fraternity. On the physical plane the present state-systems must be replaced throughout the whole world by institutions or organizations which are imbued with fraternity. On the other hand, everything that is connected with the Church and religion must be independent of external organization, state organization and organizations akin to the state; it must become the province of the soul and be developed in a completely free community. The evolution of socialism must be accompanied by complete freedom of thought in matters of religion.

Present-day socialism in the form of social democracy has declared that 'religion is a private matter'. But it observes this dictum about as much as a mad bull observes fraternity when it attacks someone. Socialism has not the slightest understanding of religious tolerance, for in its present form socialism itself is a religion; it is pursued in a sectarian spirit and displays extreme intolerance. Socialism therefore must be accompanied by a real flowering of the religious life which is founded upon the free communion of souls on earth.

Just think for a moment how radically the course of evolution has thereby been impeded. There must be opposition to evolution at first, so that one can then work for a period of time towards the furtherance of evolution; this, in its turn, will be followed by a reaction and so on. I spoke of this in discussing the general principles of history. I pointed out that nothing is permanent, everything that exists is doomed to perish. Think of the opposition to this parallel development of freedom of thought in the sphere of religion and in the sphere of external social life, a development that can only be realized within the state community! If socialism is to prevail the religious life must be completely independent of the state organization; it must inspire the hearts and souls of men who are living together in a community, completely independent of any kind of organization. What mistakes have been made in this domain! 'Christ is the Spirit'—and alongside this, the terrible ecclesiastical organization of Czarism! 'Christ is the King'—complete identification of Czarism and religious convictions!* And not only has the Roman Catholic Church established itself as a political power, it has also managed, especially in the course of recent centuries, indirectly through Jesuitism, to infiltrate the other domains, to participate in their organization and to imbue them with the spirit of Catholicism. Or take the case of Lutheranism. How has it developed? It is true that Luther was the product of that impulse† of which I have already

* Note—the stenogram is unclear.
† See 11th and 18th September, 1917, *Das Karma des Materialismus* (in Bibl. Nr. 176).

## Lecture IX

spoken here on another occasion—he is a typical Janus who turns one face to the fourth post-Atlantean epoch and the other to the fifth post-Atlantean epoch, and in this respect he is animated by an impulse in conformity with our time. Luther appears on the stage of history—but what happens then? What Luther wanted to realize in the religious sphere is associated with the interests of the petty German princes and their Courts. A prince is appointed bishop, head of synod, etcetera. Thus we see harnessed together two realms which should be completely independent of each other. Or to take another example—the state-principle which permeates the external organization of the state is impregnated with the Catholic religious principle, as was the case in Austria, the Austria which is now disintegrating; and to this, fundamentally, Austria's downfall must be attributed. Under other leadership, especially that of Goetheanism, it would have been possible to restore order in Austria.

On the other hand, amongst the English-speaking population in the West the princes and the aristocracy have everywhere infiltrated the Lodges. It is a characteristic feature of the West that one cannot understand the state organization unless we bear in mind that it is permeated with the spirit of the Lodges—and France and Italy are thoroughly infected by it—any more than one can understand Central Europe unless one realizes that it is impregnated with Jesuitism. We must bear in mind therefore that grievous mistakes have been made in respect of freedom of thought and social equality that must necessarily accompany socialism.

The development of socialism must be accompanied by another element in the sphere of the spiritual life—the emancipation of all aspiration towards the spirit, which must be independent of the state organization, and the removal of all fetters from knowledge and everything connected with knowledge. Those 'barracks' of learning called universities, which are scattered throughout the world are the greatest impediment to the evolution of the fifth post-Atlantean epoch. Just as there must be freedom in the sphere of religion, so, too, in the sphere of knowledge all must be free and equal, everyone must be able to play his part in the further development of mankind. If the socialist movement is to develop along healthy lines, privileges, patents and monopolies must be abolished in every branch of knowledge. Since, at the present time, we are still very far from understanding what I really mean, there is no need for me to show you in any way how knowledge could be freed from its fetters, and how every man could thus be induced to participate in evolution. For that will depend upon the development of far reaching impulses in the sphere of education, and in the whole relationship between man and man. Ultimately all monopolies, privileges and patents which are related to the possession of intellectual knowledge will disappear; man will have no other choice but to affirm in every way and in all domains the spiritual life that dwells in him and to express it with all the vigour at his command. At a time when there is a growing tendency for the universities, for example, to claim exclusive rights in medicine, when in widely different spheres people wish to organize everything with maximum efficiency, at such a time there is no need to discuss spiritual equality in detail, for at present this is far beyond our reach and most people can safely wait until their next incarnation before they arrive at a complete understanding of what is to be said on the subject of this third point. But the first steps of course can be undertaken at all times.

Since we are involved in the modern world and the modern epoch, all we can do is to be aware of the impulses at work, especially socialism and what must accompany it—

## Lecture IX

freedom of religious thought, equality in the sphere of knowledge. Knowledge must become equal for all, in the sense of the proverb which says that in death all men are equal, death is the great leveller; for knowledge, even as death, opens the door to the supersensible world. One can no more acquire exclusive rights for death than one can acquire exclusive rights for knowledge. To do so nevertheless is to produce not men who are vehicles of knowledge, but those who have become the so-called vehicles of knowledge at the present time. These words in no way refer to the individual; they refer to what is important for our time, namely, the social configuration of our time. Our epoch especially which saw the gradual decline of the bourgeoisie has shown how all rebellion against that which runs counter to evolution is increasingly ineffective today. The Papacy firmly sets its face against evolution. When, in the seventies, the 'Old Catholics'[8] rejected the dogma of papal infallibility, this consummation of papal absolutism, life was made difficult for them (and is still made difficult for them today); meanwhile they could render valuable service by their resistance to papal absolutism.

If you recall what I have said you will find that, at the present time, there exists on the physical plane something which in reality belongs to the soul life and to the spiritual life of men whilst on the external physical plane fraternity seeks to manifest itself. That which does belong directly to the physical plane, i.e. freedom, has manifested itself on the physical plane and has organized it. Of course in so far as men live on the physical plane and freedom dwells in the souls of men, it belongs to the physical plane; but where people are subject to organizations on this plane there is no place for freedom. On the physical plane, for example, religions must be able to be exclusively communities of souls and must be free from external organization. Schools must be organized on a different basis, and above all, they must not become state-controlled schools. Everything must be determined by freedom of thought, by individual needs. Because in the world of reality things interpenetrate it may happen that today socialism, for example, often denies its fundamental principle. It shows itself to be tyrannical, avid for power and would dearly like to take everything into its own hands. Inwardly, it is, in reality, the adversary of the unlawful prince of this world who appears when one organizes externally the Christ impulse or the spiritual in accordance with state principles, when, in the external organization, fraternity alone does not suffice.

When we discuss vital and essential questions of the contemporary world we touch upon matters which mankind finds unpalatable today. But it is important that these problems should be thoroughly understood. It is only by gaining a clear understanding of these problems that we can hope to escape from the present calamitous situation. I must repeat again and again that we shall only be able to contribute to the true evolution of mankind by acquiring knowledge of the impulses which can be found in the way I have described.

When I discussed here a week ago my book *The Philosophy of Freedom* I tried to show how, as a result of my literary activities, I was rejected everywhere. You will recall no doubt that in many fields my work met with opposition. Even when I attempted in the recent fateful years to draw attention to Goetheanism I was ignored on all sides. Goetheanism does not mean that one writes or says something on the subject of Goethe, but it is also Goetheanism to search for an answer to the question: What is the best solution, anywhere in the world at the present time, when all nations are at each others throats? But here too I felt myself ignored on all sides. I do not say this out of pessimism, for I know the workings of Karma much too well for that. Nor do I say it

## Lecture IX

because I would not do the same again tomorrow if the opportunity presented itself. I must say it because it is necessary to apprise mankind of many things, because only by insight into reality can mankind, for its part, find the impulses appropriate to the present age.

Must it then be that men will never succeed in finding the path to the 'light' by awakening that which dwells in their hearts and their inmost souls? Must they then come to the 'light' through external constraint? Must everything collapse about their ears before they begin to think? Should not this question be raised afresh every day? I do not ask that the individual shall do this or that—for I know only too well that little can be done at the present moment. But what is necessary is to have insight and understanding, to avoid false judgement and the passive attitude which refuses to see things as they really are.

A remark which I read in the *Frankfurter Zeitung* this morning made a strange impression upon me. It was an observation of a man whom I knew intimately some eighteen or twenty years ago and with whom I have discussed many different questions. I read in the *Frankfurter Zeitung* an article by this man; it was from the pen of Paul Ernst,[9] poet and dramatist, whose plays have been performed on the public stage. I knew him intimately at that time. It was a short article on *moral courage* and in it I read a sentence—it is indeed very encouraging to find such a sentence today, but one must constantly raise the question: must we suffer the present catastrophe for such a sentence to be possible? A cultured German, a man who is German to the core writes: in Germany people have always maintained that we are universally hated. I should like to know (he writes) who on earth really hated the creative genius of Germany? And then he recalls that in recent years it is the Germans themselves who have shown the greatest antipathy to the creative genius of Germany.

And in particular they harbour a real inner antipathy to Goetheanism. I do not say this in order to criticize in any way, and certainly not—you would hardly expect this of me—to say something that would in any way imply making concessions to Wilsonism. It is tragic when things happen only under constraint, whereas they could be truly beneficial if they were the fruit of freedom. For today that which must be the object of freedom must stem from free thoughts. I must constantly reiterate that I say these things not in order to evoke pessimism, but in order to appeal to your hearts and souls so that you, in your turn, may appeal to the hearts and souls of others and so awaken insight—and therefore understanding! What has suffered most in recent years is judgement that has allowed itself to be clouded by submission to authority. How happy people are, the world over, that they have a schoolmaster for their idol (i.e. Wilson), that they no longer need to think for themselves! This must not be accounted a virtue or defect of any particular nation. It is something that is now widespread and must be resisted: we must endeavour to support our judgements with sound reasoning. One does not form judgements by getting up on one's hind legs and pronouncing judgements indiscriminately. Those who are often the leading personalities today—and I have already spoken of this in a different context—are the worst possible choice, the products of the particular circumstances of our time. We must be aware of this. It is not a question of clinging to slogans such as democracy, socialism etcetera; what is important is to perceive the realities behind the words.

That is what one feels, what comes to mind at the present time when one sees so clearly that the few who are shaken out of their complacency awaken only under constraint,

## Lecture IX

when compelled to do so by constraint. That is why one says to oneself: what matters is judgement, insight and understanding. In order to gain insight into the evolution of nations we must bear in mind these deeper relationships. We must have the courage to say to ourselves: all our knowledge of ethnology and everything that is concerned with the social organization is valueless unless one is aware of these things. We must summon up the courage to say this and it is of this courage that I wanted to speak. I have spoken long enough, but I felt that it was important to show the direct connection between the deeper European impulses and those of the present time.

As you are aware one can never know from one day to the next how long one is permitted to remain in a particular place—one may be compulsorily directed at the behest of the authorities. Whatever happens—one never knows how long we may be together—in any case, though I may have to leave very soon, the present lecture will not be the last. I will see to it that I can speak to you again here in Dornach.

# NOTES

## LECTURE I

1. Carolingian and Hohenstaufen dynasties marked by the struggle between Empire and Papacy.
2. A French bishop, Clement V, is elected to the papal throne. The papal court transferred to Avignon 1309. Beginning of the 'Babylonian Captivity'.
3. Knights Templar. Founded 1118 by Hugues de Payen to protect pilgrims on their way to the Holy Sepulchre. After their defeat at Acre 1291 they took refuge in Cyprus. The order was denounced 1307 by the Inquisition; their property was sequestrated. The Templars were arrested and most, including the leader, Jacques Molay, tortured and burnt. Papal Bull 1312 suppressed the Order.
4. Mongol invasions. After destroying the power of China and Islam in Central Asia, the armies of Chingis Khan (1167-1227) advanced through Georgia, overran the Ukraine and the Crimea and destroyed three Russian armies (1222-3). A renewed invasion of Russia began in 1237 under Ögödei. The Mongols captured Moscow, Rostov, Yaroslavl and destroyed the army of the Grand Duke. In 1240 they advanced towards Poland and Hungary and reached Pesth. Another army overran Lithuania and East Prussia. Archduke Henry of Silesia was defeated at Liegnitz by a force under Kaidu and in 1241 all Hungary fell to the Mongols. The death of Ögödie in 1241 saved Western Europe from further invasion. A full account will be found in *The Mongols* by E. D. Phillips, Thames & Hudson, 1969. Also, *The Mongols and Russia* by G. Vernadsky, Yale, 1959.
5. H. T. Buckle (1822-62) English historian. His chief work was the *History of Civilisation in England* (1857-61). He saw in the law of causality the determining factor in history. Freidrich Ratzel (1844-1904). Geographer and professor in Munich and Leipzig.
6. Ernst von Wildenbruch (1845-1909). Author of historical dramas—*Die Karolinger* 1881, *Die Quitzows* 1888, etcetera. Filled with a sense of priestly mission. His plays are patriotic, rhetorical and rely upon stage effects. 'He was capable of raising a storm to put out a night light!'
7. Ottokar II (1253-78), King of Bohemia, was compelled to surrender

## From Symptom to Reality in Modern History

Austria, Styria and Carinthia to Rudolf of Hapsburg. He refused to recognize the validity of Rudolf's election as emperor and was defeated and mortally wounded at the battle of Marchfeld 1278.
8. Osmanlis or Ottomans, a western Turkish race named after their leader Osman I or Ottoman (d. 1326) who founded the Turkish empire by conquering western Asia Minor. A nomadic people.
9. Council of Constance (1414–18). John Hus was summoned to defend himself before the Church authorities against the charge of heresy. Refused to recant and was convicted and burnt.
10. Defenestration of Prague 1618. Protestant meetings prohibited by Imperial decree. Calvinists invaded the Hradschin Palace in Prague and threw the Imperial regents, Martinitz and Slavata, together with their secretary, Fabricius, out of the window on to the courtyard fifty feet below. A Bohemian rebellion now became inevitable.
11. Peace of Westphalia 1648. Religious clauses a return to the Peace of Augsburg 1565— 'cujus regio, ejus religio'. Territorial and political implications of the treaty of great significance in European history.
12. James I of England or James VI of Scotland aptly described by Henry IV of Navarre and Sully as the 'wisest fool in Christendom.'

## LECTURE II

1. Stephen I (992–1038) King of Hungary, patron saint of Hungary. He brought Hungary into the orbit of Western Culture. The 'sacred crown' is now in America.
2. Novalis (Friedrich von Hardenberg) (1772–1802). His unfinished novel *Heinrich von Ofterdingen* 1802 is an allegory of Novalis' spiritual life and was the representative novel of early Romanticism.
3. Richard Cobden (1804–54) and John Bright (1811–89), leaders of 'Manchesterism', the school of radical free trade principles.
4. German liberalism. In 1848 the German liberals attempted to establish a constitutional state and the National Assembly offered the crown to Frederick William IV who refused to meet liberal demands. Later the movement split into moderates and radicals (the German Progressive Party). Finally the National Liberals supported Bismarck's anti-clericalism and imperialism. By the end of the century liberalism was a spent force.
5. Friedrich Lassalle (1823–64), architect of the German labour movement. In his 'Open letter' 1863 he urged the proletariat to form an independent political party. Founder and president of the 'General Association of German Workers'.
6. 'The materialist conception of history starts from the principle that production, and with production the exchange of its products, is the basis of every social order ... the ultimate causes of all social

# Notes

change and political revolutions are to be sought not in the minds of men ... but in changes in the mode of production and exchange' (Marx: *Anti-Dühring*). 'The mode of production of the material means of existence conditions the whole process of social, political and intellectual life. It is not the consciousness of men that determines their existence, but it is their social existence which determines their consciousness' (Marx: Preface to the *Critique of Political Economy*). 'The division of labour implies from the outset the division of the conditions of labour, of tools and materials and thus the splitting up of accumulated capital among different owners, and thus, the division between capital and labour, and the different forms of property itself' (Marx on the class war in *The German Ideology*).

## LECTURE III

1. Frédéric Jean Soret (1795–1865). Scientist and author. A frequent visitor in Goethe's house. Notes from his journal were used by Eckermann for his 'Conversations with Goethe'.

## LECTURE IV

1. The Austrian Minister was Dr. Giskra (1820–79).
2. Oskar Hertwig (1849–1922). Director of the Anatomical-biological Institute in Berlin (1888–1921). Author of works on biology, zoology. Rejected Darwin's theory of sexual selection.

## LECTURE V

1. E. Horneffer (b. 1871). A disciple of Nietzsche, professor in Giessen. Emphasized pedagogic value of Graeco-Roman culture.

## LECTURE VI

1. Count Leopald von Kalkreuth (1855–1928). Landscape and portrait painter. Professor at the Weimar Art School, 1885–90.
2. W. Scherer (1841–86). Pioneer of philological approach to the study of literature. Professor of German languages, Berlin.
3. H. von Treitsche (1834–96). Historiographer of the Prussian state. A Patriot and nationalist. Published the *Preussische Jahrbücher* (1866–89).
4. R. Strauss (1864–1949). Director State Opera, Vienna, 1918. Famous for choral works, Lieder, chamber music, ballet and opera.

## From Symptom to Reality in Modern History

5. Woldemar von Biedermann (1817–1903). Goethe scholar. Edited a collection of Goethe's *Gespräche* (1889–96) 10 vols.
6. Kreuzwendedich Frieherr von Rheinbaben (1855–1921). 1901–9, Prussian Finance Minister; 1913–21, President of the Goethe Society.
7. Eduard von Hartmann (1842–1906). *Philosophie des Unbewussten*, 1869. See Rudolf Steiner's *The Riddles of Philosophy*, Part II and his *Briefe*, Vol II, 1953.
8. Harry Graf Kessler (1868–1937); K. Breysig (1855–1940), historian.
9. Benjamin Tucker published in America a periodical: *Liberty, the Pioneer Organ of Anarchism*. J. H. Mackay (1864–1933). Belonged to the literary Bohemia of Berlin. Popularized 'individual anarchism', cf. his novel *Die Anarchisten*, 1891. The hero is the mouthpiece of the author. An aggressive socialist. Dealt with in detail in R. Steiner's *Gesammelte Aufästze zur Kulturgeschichte* (1887–1901).
10. About the expression: 'vain self-praise stinks' Goethe commented: 'That may be; but the public has no nose for the smell of others' unjust criticism.'
11. A. Dreyfus (1859–1935). Jewish officer falsely accused of treason and transported to Devil's Island. Rehabilitated 1906.
12. W. Bölsche (1862–1939). Disciple of Zola; tried to link poetry and science. Scientific popularisor. Best known for *Das Liebesleben in der Natur*, 3 vols.
13. O. E. Hartleben (1864–1905). Dramatist, novelist and lyric poet. Attacked moral conventions and believed in the free personality.
14. M. Halbe (1865–1944). Dramatist and novelist. Nostalgia for lost youth, attachment to homeland, W. Prussia. (See R. Steiner's *Gesammelte Aufsätze zur Dramaturgie*, 1889–1900).
15. Rosa Luxemburg (1870–1919). Radical Socialist, worked for overthrow of existing regime. Opposed to war 1914. Author of 'Spartakus' letters 1916. Drafted programme of newly formed Communist party 1918. With K. Liebknecht fomented Spartakus rebellion, January, 1919. Finally shot by counter revolutionaries.
16. Theodor Herzka (1845–1924). National economist. Wished to establish settlement co-operatives in various countries, e.g. Africa, and to redistribute land in order to break the monopoly of landed proprietors.

## LECTURE VII

1. R. Hamerling (1830–89). Early work lyrical poems. *Homunculus* (1888) attacked the soullessness of the epoch. Philosophy opposed to monism and pessimism.
2. The Gymnasium prepared pupils for the Abitur and the University.

## Notes

Main subjects Greek and Latin; two foreign languages, usually French and English, included in the curriculum.
Realschule. Here emphasis on Mathematics and Natural Sciences. This type of school had a vocational bias.
3. Leitha and Leithania. The Leitha a tributary of the Danube. Up till 1918 formed the frontier between Austria and Hungary. The Austrian half of the Empire called Cis-Leithania, the Hungarian half, Trans-Leithania. See *The Hapsburg Empire* by C. S. Macartney, 1968.
4. Redemptorists. St. Alfonso de Liguori (1696–1787) founded the Congregation of the Most Holy Redeemer. Members of this congregation called Redemptionists. Undertook missionary work in the dioceses around Naples, heard confession and supervised schools. St. Alfonso beatified 1816 and canonized 1839.
5. The 'Reich German' refers to the German who was born and lived in Imperial Germany pre-1918.
6. John Calvin (1509–64). Founded the theological academy in Geneva. Taught doctrine of predestination. Ulrich Zwingli (1484–1531). Head of the Reformed Church in Switzerland. Killed in the Confessional war between Zürich and the five Cantons.
7. Gottfried Herder (1744–1807). A seminal influence in theology, history, philosophy and pedagogy. Friend of Goethe. See any history of German literature.
8. Karl von Linné or Linnaeus (1707–78). Swedish naturalist. Inventor of artificial system of plant classification.
9. Gustav Stresemann (1878–1929). National liberal politician. Post-1918 advocated a policy of reconciliation. Chancellor 1923. Foreign Minister 1923–9. Nobel Peace Prize 1926.
10. K. J. Schröer (1825–1900). Literary historian. Professor of history of literature at the Technische Hochschule in Vienna. Teacher of R. Steiner. See latter's *Course of my Life*.
11. R. Eucken (1846–1929). Professor of Philosophy, Jena. Pioneer of idealist metaphysics.
    H. Bergson (1859–1941). Professor at Collège de France. Famous for his book *Creative Evolution* and the idea of the *élan vital* as the fundamental stuff of the Universe.
12. Thomas Woodrow Wilson (1856–1924). Professor of Jurisprudence and Political Economy. President U.S.A. 1912–20. Author of the 'Fourteen Points' as basis for peace 1918. Idea of a 'League of Nations' stemmed from him; also of a world government to prevent future wars.

### LECTURE VIII

1. Photius (815–869). Patriarch of Constantinople and author of the great schism between the Orthodox Church and the Church of

Rome. This schism finally centred on the 'filioque' controversy. The Western Church added *filioque* ('and the Son') to the Constantinopolitan Creed, the so called double Procession of the Holy Ghost. Photius refused the insertion of filioque in the Nicene Creed. The Orthodox Church sees in Photius the champion of their cause against Rome. The addition of *filioque* became a dogma of the Roman Church in the fourth Lateran Council 1215.

2. Ignatius Loyola (1491–1556). Wounded at siege of Pamplona 1521 and during convalescence read devotional books. 1522 retired to Manresa, devoted himself to prayer and meditation. Sketched the fundamentals of the *Spiritual Exercises*. Took the monastic vows, gathered a few companions (e.g. Francis Xavier, Peter Favre) who became nucleus of the Society of Jesus. The *Spiritual Exercises* is a book of devotion and a training manual. Approved by Pope Paul 1540. Loyola beatified 1609, canonized 1622. See R. Fülop Müller, *Power and Secrets of the Jesuits*, 1930; Father J. Brodrick, *The Origin of the Jesuits*, 1940; and *Ignatius Loyola, the Pilgrim Years*, 1956.

3. Zwingli and Calvin—see notes to Lecture VI.

Kaspar von Schwenkfeld (1489–1561). An Evangelical sectarian. His followers formed communities in Silesia and Pennsylvania.

Anabaptists. A Christian sect of the Reformation which rejected infant baptism and believed in the establishment of the Kingdom of God on earth. Associated with the peasant revolts in Saxony 1521. Leaders executed, banished or expelled.

4. Vladimir Solovieff (1853–1900). Russian theologian, philosopher and poet. His philosophy has a profound mystical quality. Opposed to Slavophil nationalism and the despotic state. See N. Berdyaev, *The Russian Idea*, 1947. (This book useful on the interpretation of the Russian make-up, cf. Lecture I of this course); N. L. Lossky, *History of Russian Philosophy*, 1953.

5. Alexander Baumgartner (1841–1910). Catholic literary historian. Member of the Jesuit Order. His book *Goethe* 1885 emphasizes the Catholic point of view.

6. George Henry Lewes (1871–78). Best known for the *Life and Works of Goethe*, 2 vols, 1855.

## LECTURE IX

1. Arianism and Athanasianism. The doctrinal conflict between Arius (250–336) and Athanasius (d. 373) arose over the question of the divine Sonship of Christ. Arius maintained the Son was not God, that He was not of divine substance and not eternal, but a creation 'begotten of God'. Athanasius defended the Godhead of the Son. Christ was truly the Son and truly God. Arianism remained the

## Notes

official religion of the eastern half of the Roman Empire down to 378. The Athanasian doctrine, accepted by the Western Church at first, rejected by the Council of Antioch 341, but later supported by emporers Constantine II and Constans. The victory of the Nicene doctrine assured by the support of the Church Fathers, Basil of Caesarea, Gregory of Nazianzus and Gregory of Nyssa. The second Council of Constantinople 381 confirmed the Nicene faith and in 383 Arianism was proscribed. See Hastings *Encyclopedia of Religion*.

2. Ulfilas, the Teutons and the *Heliand*. The migrations of the early Christian era led to tribal groupings. The Teutonic tribes (Germanic peoples or Germans) were composed of N. Teutons, E. Teutons (Goths, Vandals and Burgundians) and W. Teutons (Franks, Saxons, Langobards).

    The 'Migration of the Peoples' (375–568) led to attacks upon the frontiers of the Roman Empire.

    Ulfilas or Wulfila (310–383). A Visigothic bishop; translated part of the Bible into Gothic. (Codex Argenteus at Uppsala.) Major influence in conversion of Visigoths to Arian christianity.

    The Langobard Kingdom in Italy lasted from 568–772.

    Clovis d. 511 captured Gaul for the Arian Visigoths. Was baptized 496, established a Frankish national church and so won support for Roman Catholicism.

    Charles the Great overthrew the Langobards, Frisians and Saxons and united Germany under a single ruler. He was crowned in St. Peters 800 by Pope Leo III. The alliance of the Papacy and the Carolingians ensured the victory of Catholic Christianity.

    Other influences in the diffusion of Christianity were the monasteries, poetic works such as the *Muspilli* (830), the *Heliand* (circa 830) in which Christ is portrayed as King and warrior, his disciples as vassals. The purpose of the poem was frankly didactic. (This complicated period of history should be studied in some standard work.)

3. *Aufklärung* or Enlightenment. A rationalist movement originating in England and associated with the names of Locke, Hobbes, Hume and Newton; in France with Voltaire and the Encyclopedists; in Germany with Lessing, Wolff, Nicolai and Kant. 'Sapere aude' said Kant—dare to be wise, have the courage to use your reason. See Kant, *Was ist Aufklärung?*

4. Lord Herbert of Cherbury (1583–1648) was called the 'father of deism'. The five propositions in *De Veritate* 1624 were tenets of 'natural religion'. He wished to show that Christianity and its doctrines were reasonable.

5. John Locke (1632–1704). In philosophy an empiricist; forerunner of the Enlightenment. See *An Essay Concerning Human Understanding*, 1690.

## From Symptom to Reality in Modern History

Thomas Hobbes (1588–1679). Philosopher: mathematical-mechanical conception of nature. Universe and man envisaged as complex machines. Politically, he looked to enlightened despotism; cf. *Leviathan*, 1651.

6. A. van Harnack (1851–1930). Protestant theologian and exegete; leading patristic scholar of the nineteenth century. Chief of the liberal Ritschl school of theology. Followed scientific-historical method, emphasis on 'source study'. *History of Dogma*, 7 vols.; *What is Christianity?*
7. M. A. Bakunin (1814–76). Russian revolutionary and anarchist. Co-founder of the first International.
8. The Old Catholics. Party of reform in the R. C. Church who rejected the doctrine of papal infallibility and of Immaculate Conception. Movement founded by Döllinger in Munich 1871.
9. Paul Ernst (1866–1933). Neo-classic poet, novelist and dramatist. Strove to unite classical form and modern thought; cf. *Der Weg zur Form*, 1906. Wrote books connected with the war and its aftermath, *Der Zusammenbruch des deutschen Idealismus*, 1920.

Short list of relevant works by Rudolf Steiner, published or distributed by *Rudolf Steiner Press*, though not necessarily all in print at any one time:

*The Philosophy of Freedom*
*The Course of my Life*
*The Spiritual Guidance of Man and Mankind*
*Mysticism and Modern Thought*
*Goethe's Conception of the World*
*A Theory of Knowledge implicit in Goethe's World Conception*
*World History in the Light of Anthroposophy*

All the published works of Rudolf Steiner in print in English as well as the works of other authors on Anthroposophy, can be obtained from Rudolf Steiner Press, 35 Park Road, London, NW1 6XT. Catalogue available.

## COMPLETE EDITION

of the works of Rudolf Steiner in the original German. Published by the *Rudolf Steiner Verlag*, 4143, Dornach, Switzerland.

*General Plan (abbreviated)*:

### A. WRITINGS

I. Works written between 1883 and 1925
II. Essays and articles written between 1882 and 1925
III. Letters, drafts, manuscripts, fragments, verses, inscriptions, meditative sayings, etc.

### B. LECTURES

I. Public Lectures
II. Lectures to Members of the Anthroposophical Society on general anthroposophical subjects
III. Lectures and Courses on special branches of work:
   Art: Eurythmy, Speech and Drama, Music, Visual Arts, History of Art
   Education
   Medicine and Therapy
   Science
   Sociology and the Threefold Social Order
   Lectures given to Workmen at the Goetheanum

The total number of lectures amounts to some six thousand, shorthand reports of which are available in the case of the great majority.

### C. REPRODUCTIONS and SKETCHES

Paintings in water colour, drawings, coloured diagrams, Eurythmy forms, etc.

A full and detailed *Bibliographical Survey*, with subjects, dates and places where the lectures were given, is available.

All the volumes can be obtained direct from the Rudolf Steiner Verlag (address as above) or from the Rudolf Steiner and other bookshops in this country.